BLEU
1

McDOUGAL LITTELL

Discovering
FRENCH
Nouveau!

Unit 2 Resource Book

Components authored by Jean-Paul Valette and Rebecca M. Valette:

- Workbook
- Communipak
- Assessment Program
- Video Program
- Audio Program

Components authored by Sloane Publications:

- Family Letter, *Patricia Smith*
- Absent Student Copymasters, *E. Kristina Baer*
- Family Involvement, *Patricia Smith*
- Multiple Choice Test Items, *Nicole Dicop-Hineline*

Other Components

- Video Activities, *T. Jeffrey Richards, Philip D. Korfe, Consultant*
- Comprehensive (Semester) Tests, *T. Jeffrey Richards*
- Activités pour tous, *Patricia L. Ménard*

ISBN: 0 - 618 - 29827 - 4

2 3 4 5 6 7 8 9 — MDO — 07 06 05 04 03

Table of Contents
Unité 2. La vie courante

To the Teacher

The Unit Resource Books that accompany each unit of *Discovering French, Nouveau!–Bleu* provide a wide variety of materials to practice, expand on, and assess the material in the *Discovering French, Nouveau!–Bleu* student text.

Components

Following is a list of components included in each Unit Resource Book, correlated to each **Leçon:**
- Workbook, Teacher's Edition
- *Activités pour tous*, Teacher's Edition
- Lesson Plans
- Block Scheduling Lesson Plans
- Family Letter
- Absent Student Copymasters
- Family Involvement
- Video Activities
- Videoscripts
- Audioscripts
- Lesson Quizzes

Unit Resources include the following materials:
- Communipak
- *Activités pour tous* Reading, Teacher's Edition
- Workbook Reading and Culture Activities, Teacher's Edition
- Lesson Plans for *Images*
- Block Scheduling Lesson Plans for *Images*
- Assessment
    Unit Test
    Listening Comprehension Performance Test
    Speaking Performance Test
    Reading Comprehension Performance Test
    Writing Performance Test
    Multiple Choice Test Items
    Test Scoring Tools

- Audioscripts
- Videoscripts for *Images*
- Answer Key

Component Description

Workbook, Teacher's Edition

The *Discovering French, Nouveau!–Bleu* Workbook directly references the student text. It provides additional practice to allow students to build their control of French and develop French proficiency. The activities provide guided communicative practice in meaningful contexts and frequent opportunity for self-expression.

Listening Activities give students the opportunity to demonstrate comprehension of spoken French in a variety of realistic contexts. Students listen to excerpts from the CD that accompanies the *Discovering French, Nouveau!–Bleu* program while working through listening activities to improve both general and discrete comprehension skills.

Writing Activities give students the chance to develop their writing skills and put into practice what they have learned in class. The last activity is called *Communication* and encourages students to express themselves in various additional communicative situations.

The Reading and Culture Activities contain realia (illustrations and objects from real life) from French-speaking countries and various kinds of cultural activities. Each unit includes one set of Reading and Culture Activities.

Activités pour tous, Teacher's Edition

The activities in *Activités pour tous* include vocabulary, grammar, and reading practice at varying levels of difficulty. Each practice section is three pages long, with each page corresponding to a level of difficulty (A, B, and C). A is the easiest and C is the most challenging.

Lesson Plans

These lesson plans follow the general sequence of a *Discovering French, Nouveau!–Bleu* lesson. Teachers using these plans should become familiar with both the overall structure of a *Discovering French, Nouveau!–Bleu* lesson and with the format of the lesson plans and available ancillaries before translating these plans to a daily sequence.

Block Scheduling Lesson Plans

These plans are structured to help teachers maximize the advantages of block scheduling, while minimizing the challenges of longer periods.

Family Letter and Family Involvement

This section offers strategies and activities to increase family support for students' study of French language and culture.

Absent Student Copymasters

The Absent Student Copymasters enable students who miss part of a **Leçon** to go over the material on their own. The Absent Student Copymasters also offer strategies and techniques to help students understand new or challenging information. If possible, make a copy of the CD, video, or DVD available, either as a loan to an absent student or for use in the school library or language lab.

Video Activities and Videoscript

The Video Activities that accompany the Video or DVD for each module focus students' attention on each video section and reinforce the material presented in the module. A transcript of the Videoscript is included for each **Leçon.**

Audioscripts

This section provides scripts for the Audio Program and includes vocabulary presentations, dialogues, readings and reading summaries, audio for Workbook and Student Text activities, and audio for Lesson Quizzes.

Communipak

The Communication section contains five types of oral communication activities introduced sequentially by level of challenge or difficulty. Designed to encourage students to use French for communication in conversational exchanges, they include *Interviews*, *Tu as la parole*, *Conversations*, *Échanges*, and *Tête à tête* activities.

Assessment

Lesson Quizzes

The Lesson Quizzes provide short accuracy-based vocabulary and structure assessments. They measure how well students have mastered the new conversational phrases, structures, and vocabulary in the lesson. Also designed to encourage students to review material in a given lesson before continuing further in the unit, the quizzes provide an opportunity for focused cyclical re-entry and review.

Unit Tests

The Unit Tests are intended to be administered upon completion of each unit. They may be given in the language laboratory or in the classroom. The total possible score for each test is 100 points. Scoring suggestions for each section appear on the test sheets. The Answer Key for the Unit Tests appears at the end of the Unit Resource Book.

There is one Unit Test for each of the eight units in *Discovering French, Nouveau!–Bleu*. Each test is available in two versions: Form A and Form B. A complete Audioscript is given for the listening portion of the tests; the recordings of these sections appear on CDs 13–16.

Speaking Performance Test

These tests enable teachers to evaluate students' comprehension, ability to respond in French, and overall fluency. Designed to be administered to students individually, each test consists of two sections, *Conversations* and *Tu as la parole*.

Reading Comprehension Performance Test

These tests allow for evaluation of students' ability to understand material written in French. The Reading Comprehension Performance Test is designed for group administration. Each test contains several reading selections, in a variety of styles. Each selection is accompanied by one to four related multiple-choice questions in English.

Listening Comprehension Performance Test

The Listening Comprehension Test is designed for group administration. Each test contains ten short listening items, each accompanied by a multiple-choice question. The test is divided into two parts, *Conversations* and *Questions et réponses*. The listening selections are recorded on CD, and the full script is also provided so that the teacher can administer the test either by playing the CD or by reading the selections aloud.

Writing Performance Test

The Writing Performance Test gives students the opportunity to demonstrate how well they can use the material in the unit for self-expression. The emphasis is not on the production of specific grammar forms, but rather on the communication of meaning. Each test contains several guided writing activities, which vary in format from unit to unit.

Multiple Choice Test Items

These are the print version of the multiple choice questions from the Test Generator. They are contextualized and focus on vocabulary, grammar, reading, writing, and cultural knowledge.

Answer Key

The Answer Key includes answers that correspond to the following material:

- Video Activities
- Lesson Quizzes
- Communipak Activities
- Unit Tests
- Comprehensive Tests
- Performance Tests
- Multiple Choice Test Items

Nom _____

Classe _____ Date _____

Discovering
FRENCH
Nouveau!
B L E U

Unité 2
Leçon 3

Workbook TE

Unité 2. La vie courante

LEÇON 3   Bon appétit!   Vidéo-scène A. Tu as faim?

LISTENING ACTIVITIES

Section 1. Au café

A. Compréhension orale

a. <u> 3 </u>trois croissants   **b.** <u> 4 </u>une glace à la vanille   **c.** <u> 2 </u>un hot dog

d. <u> 1 </u>un sandwich   **e.** <u> 6 </u>un sandwich au jambon et
un sandwich au pâté   **f.** <u> 5 </u>un steak-frites et
une salade

B. Écoutez et répétez.

1. un croissant 2. un sandwich 3. un steak 4. un steak-frites 5. un hamburger 6. un hot dog

7. une salade 8. une pizza 9. une omelette 10. une crêpe 11. une glace

Nom _____

Classe _____ Date _____

Discovering FRENCH *Nouveau!*

B L E U

C. Questions et réponses

▶ Je voudrais un sandwich.

    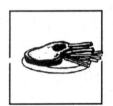

1. Je voudrais
une pizza.

2. Je voudrais
une salade.

3. Je voudrais
un hamburger.

4. Je voudrais
un croissant.

5. Je voudrais
un steak-frites.

Section 2. Intonation

D. Écoutez et répétez.

Écoutez: **Voici un steak . . . et une salade.**

Répétez: **Je voudrais une pizza.**

Je voudrais une pizza et un sandwich.

Je voudrais une pizza, un sandwich et un hamburger.

Voici un steak.

Voici un steak et une salade.

Voici un steak, une salade et une glace.

Section 3. Dictée

E. Écoutez et écrivez.

—Oh là là! J'ai _faim_ !

—Qu'est-ce que tu _veux_ ? Un steak ou _une_ pizza?

— _Donne_ -moi un steak, s'il _te_ plaît.

Nom _____

Classe _____ Date _____

Discovering
FRENCH
Nouveau!

BLEU

Unité 2
Leçon 3 Workbook TE

WRITING ACTIVITIES

1. *Un ou une?*

Complete the names of the following foods with **un** or **une**, as appropriate.

 1. _un_ sandwich

 2. _une_ pizza

 3. _un_ steak

 4. _une_ crêpe

 5. _un_ steak-frites

 6. _une_ salade

 7. _un_ croissant

 8. _une_ omelette

2. Conversations

Complete the conversations with expressions from the box.

1. —Tu as faim?

   —Oui, _j'ai_____ faim.

2. —Qu'est-ce que _tu veux_____?

   —Je _voudrais_____ une glace.

3. —S'il te plaît, _donne-moi_____ un sandwich.

   —Voilà un sandwich.

   —_Merci_____!

merci
tu veux
j'ai
je voudrais
donne-moi

---

*F*LASH culturel

Camembert, Brie, and Roquefort are all products of French origin.
What are they?

❏ pastries   ☑ cheeses   ❏ perfumes   ❏ crackers   **➔page 32**

Unité 2
Leçon 3

Workbook TE

Discovering
FRENCH *Nouveau!*

BLEU

Nom _____

Classe _____ Date _____

3. 👥 Communication: En français! (sample answers)

A. You have invited your French friend Philippe to your home.

1. *Ask Philippe if he is hungry.*

   Tu as faim, Philippe? _____

2. *Ask him if he wants a sandwich.*

   Tu veux un sandwich? _____

3. *Ask him if he wants an ice cream cone.*

   Tu veux une glace? _____

B. You are in a French restaurant with a friend.

1. *Tell your friend that you are hungry.*

   J'ai faim. _____

2. *Tell her what type of food you would like to have.*

   Je voudrais [une omelette et une salade]. _____

FLASH **culturel**

France produces over 400 varieties of cheese, among which **Camembert**, **Brie**, and **Roquefort** are the best known. In a traditional French meal, cheese is served as a separate course, after the salad and before the dessert. It is eaten with bread, and occasionally with butter.

Nom _____

Classe _____ Date _____

Discovering
FRENCH *Nouveau!*

B L E U

Unité 2
Leçon 3

Workbook TE

Vidéo-scène B. Au café

LISTENING ACTIVITIES

Section 1. Au café

A. Écoutez et répétez.

1. un soda   2. un jus d'orange   3. un jus de pomme   4. un jus de tomate   5. un jus de raisin

6. une limonade   7. un café   8. un thé   9. un chocolat

Section 2. S'il te plaît, donne-moi . . .

B. Questions et réponses

▶ —Tu veux un café ou un thé?
  —S'il te plaît, donne-moi un café.

| 1 | 2 | 3 | 4 |

S'il te plaît,   . . . un jus   . . . un jus   . . . un chocolat.
donne-moi un soda.   de tomate.   de pomme.

Nom _____

Classe _____ Date _____

Discovering
FRENCH
Nouveau!

B L E U

Section 3. Je voudrais . . .

C. Questions et réponses

▶—Vous désirez?
—Je voudrais un thé, s'il vous plaît.

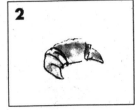

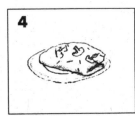

| **1** | **2** | **3** | **4** |

. . . un jus d'orange,
s'il vous plaît.

. . . un croissant,
s'il vous plaît.

. . . un steak-frites,
s'il vous plaît.

. . . une omelette,
s'il vous plaît.

Section 4. Conversations

D. Compréhension orale

1. How does the boy feel?
   a. tired
   b. thirsty
   c. hungry

2. What would the girl like?
   a. a soda
   b. a glass of orange juice
   c. a glass of grape juice

3. Where does the scene take place?
   a. in a café
   b. at a picnic
   c. at home

4. Where does the scene take place?
   a. in a café
   b. in a French restaurant
   c. at a picnic

Section 5. Dictée

E. Écoutez et écrivez.

—Vous _desirez_, mademoiselle?

—Je _voudrais_ un chocolat.

—Et vous, monsieur?

—_Donnez_-moi un _thé_, s'il _vous_ plaît.

Nom _____

Classe _____ Date _____

Discovering FRENCH *Nouveau!*

B L E U

Unité 2
Leçon 3

Workbook TE

WRITING ACTIVITIES

1. Les boissons

Find the French names of eight beverages in the following grid. The names can be read horizontally, vertically, or diagonally. Then list these beverages, using **un** or **une**, as appropriate.

J	O	J	B	M	N	C	I	X	Y	A	Z
M	U	U	R	E	W	H	L	Q	B	C	F
J	U	S	D	E	T	O	M	A	T	E	R
K	V	D	D	L	G	C	C	U	K	N	Z
X	D	E	A	E	L	O	H	T	L	Z	C
Y	B	P	A	F	R	L	C	H	X	T	P
Z	S	O	D	A	C	A	F	É	J	M	B
O	N	M	C	K	B	T	I	N	K	A	Y
L	I	M	O	N	A	D	E	S	D	O	C
S	Q	E	T	F	I	P	D	V	I	G	L
H	T	W	M	R	O	S	Y	I	U	N	J

- un soda
- un jus de pomme
- un jus de tomate
- un jus de raisin
- une limonade
- un café
- un thé
- un chocolat

2. Mes préférences (sample answers)

In the chart below, list which three of the above beverages you like the best and which three you like the least.

1. un jus de pomme
2. un chocolat
3. une limonade

4. un café
5. un jus de tomate
6. un thé

FLASH culturel

Which of the following beverages is most likely to be served with a French meal?

☐ milk   ☐ coffee   ☐ iced tea   ☑ mineral water

➡ page 36

URB
p. 7

Unité 2
Leçon 3

Workbook TE

Nom _____

Classe _____ Date _____

Discovering
FRENCH
Nouveau!

B L E U

3. Communication: En français! (sample answers)

A. Your French friend Marc has dropped by your house.

1. *Ask him if he is thirsty.*

   Tu as soif?

2. *Ask him if he wants a soda or a glass of orange juice.*

   Tu veux un soda ou un jus d'orange?

B. You are in a French café with a friend.

1. *Tell your friend that you are thirsty.*

   J'ai soif.

2. *Tell the waiter (or waitress) to bring you a beverage of your choice.*

   S'il vous plaît, donnez-moi [un jus de raisin].

FLASH culturel

The French drink a lot of mineral water. In fact, they have the highest consumption of mineral water in the world: about 60 liters per person per year. These mineral waters, some plain and some carbonated, come from natural springs in various parts of the country and are widely exported.

Nom _____

Classe _____ Date _____

Discovering FRENCH *Nouveau!*

BLEU

Unité 2
Leçon 3

Workbook TE

Vidéo-scène C. Ça fait combien?

LISTENING ACTIVITIES

Section 1. L'euro

A. Écoutez et répétez.

un euro	six euros
deux euros	sept euros
trois euros	huit euros
quatre euros	neuf euros
cinq euros	dix euros

Section 2. C'est combien?

B. Compréhension orale

Modèle	1.	2.	3.	4.	5.
10 €	6 €	8 €	19 €	22 €	35 €

C. Questions et réponses

Café des Sports

Sandwich 3€00

Soda 2€00

1. Ça fait 6 euros.   2. ...5 euros.   3. ...8 euros.   4. ...10 euros.

URB
p. 9

Nom _____

Classe _____ Date _____

Discovering
FRENCH
Nouveau!

B L E U

Section 3. Conversations

D. Compréhension orale Listening comprehension

1. What does the boy do?
   a. He orders a pizza.
   b. He asks the price of a pizza.
   c. He asks where the pizzeria is.

2. What does the woman want to do?
   a. pay the bill
   b. order food
   c. go to a café

3. What does the boy want to do?
   a. pay the bill
   b. borrow money
   c. leave a tip for the server

Section 4. Dictée.

E. Écoutez et écrivez.

—Combien coûte l'omelette?

—Elle coûte trois euros cinquante.

—Et la glace?

—Deux euros cinquante.

—Ça fait six euros au total.

   Dis, Mélanie, prête-moi six euros, s'il te plaît.

Nom _____

Classe _____ Date _____

Discovering
FRENCH
Nouveau!

BLEU

Unité 2
Leçon 3

Workbook TE

WRITING ACTIVITIES

1. C'est combien?

Identify the items pictured and give their prices.

▶ Voici un sandwich.

Il coûte deux euros.

1.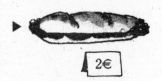

Voici un croissant.

Il coûte un euro.

2.

Voici une omelette.

Elle coûte trois euros cinquante.

3.

Voici une glace.

Elle coûte trois euros trente-cinq.

4.

Voici un steak-frites.

Il coûte six euros quarante-cinq.

5.

Voici une salade.

Elle coûte deux euros vingt.

6.

Voici un hamburger.

Il coûte quatre euros soixante.

FLASH culturel

The backs of the euro bills are illustrated with pictures of bridges.
Which bill has the most modern bridge?

❑ 10 euro note ❑ 50 euro note ❑ 100 euro note ☑ 500 euro note ➡ **page 40**

Unité 2
Leçon 3

Workbook TE

Nom _____

Classe _____ Date _____

Discovering
FRENCH
Nouveau!

B L E U

2. 👥 Communication: En français! *(sample answers)*

Imagine that you are at Le Rallye with two French friends, Olivier and Valérie.

Use the menu to write out the following conversation (in French, of course!).

Le Rallye

Boissons		Sandwichs	
Café	2€	Sandwich au jambon	3€50
Thé	2€	Sandwich au fromage	3€50
Chocolat	2€50	**Et aussi:**	
Soda	2€50	Croissant	2€
Limonade	2€25	Pizza	8€
Jus d'orange	2€50	Salade	3€50
Eau minérale	1€50	Omelette	4€50
Glaces		Hamburger	4€
Glace au café	2€50	Steak	7€
Glace à la vanille	2€50	Steak-Frites	8€50

LE GARÇON: Vous désirez?

May I help you?

TOI: Je voudrais [un sandwich au jambon et une limonade].

I would like [a food and a beverage].

VALÉRIE: Donnez-moi [un croissant et un thé], s'il vous plaît.

Please give me [a food and a beverage].

OLIVIER: Je voudrais [une glace à la vanille et un soda], s'il vous plaît.

I would like a [a food and a beverage], please.

TOI: Ça fait combien?

How much does that come to?

LE GARÇON: Ça fait [quatorze euros soixante-quinze].

That comes to [the price of what was ordered].

TOI: Dis, Olivier, prête-moi dix euros, s'il te plaît.

Hey, Olivier, loan me ten euros, please.

𝐅LASH culturel

The bills are sequenced so that the styles of bridges go from the oldest (5 euro note) to the most modern (500 euro note).

Nom _____

Classe _____ Date _____

Discovering
FRENCH *Nouveau!*
B L E U

Unité 2
Leçon 3A

Activités pour tous TE

Unité 2. La vie courante

LEÇON 3A Tu as faim?

A

Activité 1 Les articles

Select the correct articles.

1. (le)/ la / l' croissant
3. le / la /(l')omelette
5. (le)/ la / l' steak-frites

2. le /(la)/ l' pizza
4. (le)/ la / l' hamburger
6. le /(la)/ l' glace

Activité 2 Qu'est-ce que c'est?

Identify the following foods using the correct articles. Ex.: _un sandwich_

	steak-frites	glace	omelette	salade	

1. _une omelette_
3. _un steak-frites_

2. _une salade_
4. _une glace_

Activité 3 Dialogue

Select the words that best complete the following dialogue.

—Bernard, (tu as)/ j'ai faim?
—(Oui)/ non, j'ai faim.
—Qu'est-ce que (tu veux)/ je voudrais?
—Tu veux /(Je voudrais) un hamburger, une salade et une glace.
—Oh là là. (Tu as) / J'ai vraiment faim, Bernard.

B

Activité 1 Questions

Select the correct question for each response.

1. Q: _Qu'est-ce que tu veux?_

   R: Un croissant.

2. Q: _Tu as faim?_

   R: Oui, très! Et toi?

3. Q: _Tu veux un sandwich?_

   R: Oui, merci beaucoup!

Tu as faim?

Tu veux un sandwich?

Qu'est-ce que tu veux?

Nom _____

Classe _____ Date _____

Activité 2 Dialogue

Circle the statements that best complete the dialogue.

—Tu as faim?
—Non, merci. / *Oui, j'ai faim.*
—Qu'est-ce que tu veux, une crêpe ou un sandwich?
—*Je voudrais un sandwich, s'il te plaît.* / Oui, merci, j'ai faim.
—Tu veux aussi une glace?
—J'ai très faim! / *Oui, donne-moi une glace.*

Activité 3 Les repas

You are in Paris: select the foods that you eat for breakfast, lunch, and dinner.

steak-frites   croissant   salade   sandwich au jambon   glace

1. _un croissant_____

2. _un sandwich au jambon_ et
   _une glace_____

3. _un steak-frites_____ et
   _une salade_____

C

Activité 1 Questions

Write a logical question for each response.

1. _Tu as faim?_____

   Oui, j'ai faim.

2. _Qu'est-ce que tu veux?_____

   Donne-moi un sandwich au jambon, s'il te plaît.

Activité 2 Les articles indéfinis

Write the appropriate word for "a" before each word.

Modèle: un hot dog et une pizza

1. _un_____ steak et _une_____ salade
2. _un_____ sandwich et _une_____ glace

3. _un_____ hamburger et _une_____ crêpe
4. _un_____ croissant ou _une_____ omelette

Activité 3 La nourriture

Request or offer the following foods, using the right form of address.

1. (Virginie) (you offer) _Est-ce que tu veux une glace?_____

2. (Waiter) (you ask) _Je voudrais / Donnez-moi un steak-frites, s'il vous plaît._

3. (Bruno) (you ask) _Donne-moi un sandwich, s'il te plaît._

Nom _____

Classe _____ Date _____

Discovering FRENCH *Nouveau!*

BLEU

Unité 2
Leçon 3B

Activités pour tous TE

LEÇON 3B Au café

A

Activité 1 Dialogue

Select the words that best complete the dialogue.

—Tu as _soif_____ ?

—Oui, très. Je _voudrais_____ une limonade.

—Tu as _faim_____ aussi?

—Oui. S'il te plaît, _donne-moi_____ un sandwich au jambon.

| soif |
| voudrais |
| donne-moi |
| faim |

Activité 2 Formules de politesse

Are the phrases spoken to a friend (a) or to someone you don't know well (b)?

_b_ 1. Donnez-moi . . .   _b_ 4. Vous désirez?   _b_ 7. S'il vous plaît!

_a_ 2. S'il te plaît!   _a_ 5. Qu'est-ce que tu veux?   _a_ 8. Tu as soif?

_b_ 3. Excusez-moi.   _a_ 6. Donne-moi . . .

Activité 3 Les boissons

Select the drinks that people in France would logically choose in the following situations.

une limonade   un café   un jus de raisin   un chocolat

1. The children have just come in from building a snowman. _un chocolat_____

2. It's August and two friends have just played tennis. _une limonade_____

3. The family has just finished lunch. _un café_____

B

Activité 1 Dialogue

Circle the words that best complete the dialogue.

—Bonjour, mademoiselle. Vous désirez?

—J'ai bien soif. (Une limonade) / Une crêpe, s'il vous plaît.

—Et pour vous, monsieur?

—Je voudrais un café / (une pizza.) J'ai très faim!

—Et avec ça?

—Donne-moi / (Donnez-moi) un soda, s'il vous plaît.

Activité 2 La bonne réponse

Match the following questions with the appropriate responses.

_c_ 1. Vous désirez?   a. Non, c'est pour moi.

_b_ 2. On va dans un café?   b. Oui, d'accord.

_a_ 3. C'est pour vous, madame?   c. Un croissant et un café, s'il vous plaît.

Nom _____

Classe _____ Date _____

Activité 3 Les boissons (sample answers)

Identify each food and drink. Then circle the drink you'd prefer with each food.

Modèle: *un chocolat*   *un pizza*   *un soda*

1. un jus de raisin   une salade   un thé

2. un jus de tomate   une omelette   un chocolat

3. un thé   un steak-frites   une limonade

C

Activité 1 Les boissons (sample answers)

Imagine you are in a café with a friend at the following times. Order food and drinks for both of you, making selections from the illustrations in the activity above.

1. 12:30 _Pour moi, une omelette et un soda, et pour ma copine, une salade et une limonade_

2. 18:00 _Pour moi, un steak-frites et une salade, et pour mon copain, une pizza et une salade._

Activité 2 Questions et réponses

Write responses to the following comments or questions.

1. Tu as soif? _Oui, j'ai soif._

2. On va dans un café? _Oui, d'accord._

3. Vous désirez, mademoiselle/monsieur? _Je voudrais un/e..._

Activité 3 Au café

Complete the following dialogue.

Serveur: _Vous désirez?_

Anna: Je voudrais une limonade, s'il vous plaît.

Serveur: _Et pour Monsieur?_

Paul: Pour moi, un sandwich au jambon.

Serveur: _Et avec ça?_

Paul: Un jus d'orange, s'il vous plaît.

Nom _____

Classe _____ Date _____

Discovering FRENCH *Nouveau!*

B L E U

Unité 2
Leçon 3C
Activités pour tous TE

LEÇON 3C Ça fait combien?

A

Activité 1 Dialogue

Circle words to complete the dialogue.

—Combien coûte le hamburger?
—(Il) / Elle coûte 5 €.
—Et la glace?
—Il / (Elle) coûte 2 €.
—C'est combien, le jus de pomme et le café?
—(Ça fait) / Prête-moi 10 €.

Activité 2 Le bon prix

Estimate the total price of each food order.

_b_ 1. une glace   ___ a. 7 €

_a_ 2. un hamburger et   ___ b. 3 €
         un soda
                                      c. 14 €
_d_ 3. un steak-frites, une
         salade et un café   ___ d. 21 €

_c_ 4. deux pizzas et deux jus de pomme

Activité 3 C'est combien?

Write the prices in full.

1.
6€25

six euros vingt-cinq

2.
5€20

cinq euros vingt

3.
2€05

deux euros cinq

B

Activité 1 Dialogue

Circle words to complete the dialogue.

—(Combien coûte) / Voici le sandwich?
—(Il coûte) / Prête-moi cinq euros.
—Donne-moi / (Donnez-moi) aussi un jus de raisin. C'est combien?
—(Ça fait) / Combien coûte sept euros quarante.

Activité 2 Phrases à compléter

Match the first part of each sentence with its most logical conclusion.

_c_ 1. Voyons, une limonade et une pizza, . . .   a. 10 €, s'il te plaît.

_a_ 2. Dis, Karine, prête-moi . . .   b. je voudrais une omelette et un café.

_d_ 3. Zut! Où est . . .   c. ça fait 9 €.

_b_ 4. S'il vous plaît, monsieur, . . .   d. mon porte-monnaie?

Activité 3 Au menu

Estimate and write in full the correct price for each order.

 12 €   4 € 50   3 €

1.

Ça fait _trois euros._.

2.

Ça fait _douze euros._.

3.

Ça fait _quatre euros cinquante._.

Nom _____

Classe _____ Date _____

Discovering
FRENCH
Nouveau!

B L E U

C

Activité 1 Les prix

Write out how much each item costs, using **il** or **elle**.

1.   *Il coûte deux euros vingt.*

3.   *Il coûte deux euros*
   quarante.

2.   *Il coûte six euros*
   soixante-quinze

4.   *Il coûte quatre euros*
   vingt-cinq.

Activité 2 Ça fait combien?

As each person orders, tell them how much they will have to pay.

1.

2.

3.

Anna
Ça fait dix euros quarante.

Philippe
Ça fait sept euros
cinquante.

Marc
Ça fait neuf euros
soixante-quinze.

Activité 3 S'il te plaît . . .

Your friends all ask you to lend them money to make up their totals! Fill in the blanks.

1.

   —J'ai 5 €.   *Prête-moi un euro*
   cinquante, s'il te plaît.

3.
   —J'ai 5 € 50.   *Prête-moi 70 centimes,*
   s'il te plaît.

2.

   —J'ai 2 € 50.   *Prête-moi deux euros,*
   s'il te plaît.

4.
   —J'ai 4 € 25.   *Prête-moi un euro*
   vingt-cinq, s'il te plaît.

Discovering
FRENCH
Nouveau!

B L E U

Unité 2
Leçon 3

Lesson Plans

LEÇON 3A Tu as faim?, page 44

Objectives

Communicative Functions and Topics	To say you are hungry
	To offer a friend something
	To ask a friend for something
	To talk about foods
Linguistic Goals	To use *un (sandwich)* and *une (pizza)* to understand masculine and feminine nouns
	To recognize and repeat intonation
Cultural Goals	To become aware of what kinds of fast foods French young people buy

Motivation and Focus

❑ To introduce the unit, have students look at the opener on pages 42–43. Ask them to suggest what types of food might be served at the places in the pictures. Encourage students to share prior knowledge of *cafés* and *boulangeries*. Read aloud the *Introduction culturelle.*

❑ Play **Video** 3a.3 or read the **Videoscript** for *Qu'est-ce qu'on mange?* Do the CROSS-CULTURAL OBSERVATION, page 44 of the TE.

Presentation and Explanation

❑ *Lesson Opener:* To present the opening conversations, model or play **Video** 3a.1 or **Audio** CD 1, Tracks 28–29. Then have students read the conversations; ask them to imagine what is being said. Share the information in the PHOTO CULTURE NOTE on page 45 of the TE.

❑ *Pour communiquer:* Use **Overhead Transparency** 10 to present the food names and expressions in the box on page 45.

❑ *Note culturelle:* Have students read *Les jeunes et la nourriture* on page 45. Discuss differences and similarities between what French teenagers and American teenagers eat.

❑ *Petit commentaire:* Read about French sandwiches on page 46. Share the additional information in the TE margin. Students may want to compare other American and French food items such as bread.

❑ *Grammar:* Briefly explain masculine and feminine articles and nouns in the grammar box, page 46. Revisit **Overhead Transparency** 10 to reinforce article and noun agreement.

❑ *Prononciation:* Point out intonation patterns in the box, page 47. Play **Audio** CD 1, Track 30 and have students repeat.

Guided Practice and Checking Understanding

❑ Practice food vocabulary with **Overhead Transparency** 10.

❑ To check understanding, have students do **Workbook** Listening Activities A–E on pages 29–30 as they listen to the **Audioscript** or play **Audio** CD 6, Tracks 1–5.

❑ Play the **Video** or read the **Videoscript** and have students do pages 38–40 in the **Video Activities**.

❑ Model and reinforce students' listening skills with the COMPREHENSION Activity, page 45 of the TE.

Independent Practice

❑ Have students practice ordering food with the Activities on pages 46–47. Activities 2 and 4 can be completed for homework. Model Activities 1 and 3 before having students practice the dialogues in pairs.

❑ Have students work in small groups to do Activity 5 on page 41 of the **Video Activities**.

❑ Have students do any appropriate activities in **Activités pour tous,** pages 17–18.

Monitoring and Adjusting

❑ Students can do Writing Activities 1–3 on pages 31–32 of the **Workbook**.

❑ As students work on the whole-class and pair activities, monitor pronunciation and use of articles *un* and *une*. Refer students to grammar and intonation boxes on pages 46–47. Use SOUNDING FRENCH on page 47 of the TE.

Reteaching

❑ Help students redo any activities in the **Workbook** with which they had difficulty.

❑ Students can use the **Video** to review portions of the lesson.

❑ Reteach masculine and feminine nouns with the LISTENING PRACTICE Activity at the bottom of page 46 of the TE.

Summary and Closure

❑ Use **Overhead Transparency** S7 and the activities on page A14 to have students demonstrate talking about foods, asking if someone is hungry, and asking for something. You may videotape the demonstrations for inclusion in students' Oral Portfolios.

LEÇON 3B Au café, page 48

Objectives

Communicative Functions and Topics	To identify beverages To say that you are thirsty To order a beverage in a café To request something from a friend and from an adult
Linguistic Goals	To use *s'il te plaît* and *s'il vous plaît* To stress final syllables of words or groups of words
Cultural Goals	To learn about *le café*

Motivation and Focus

❑ Ask students to look at the photos on pages 48–49; encourage them to describe the places and make comparisons to their own favorite eating places. Discuss with the class favorite beverages and places to go to get something to drink.

❑ Show the **Video** or read the **Videoscript** for section 3b.3.

Presentation and Explanation

❑ *Lesson Opener:* Do the WARM-UP AND REVIEW activity, page 48 of the TE, to review forms of address. Act out or present the opening conversations with **Video** 3b.1 or **Audio** CD 1, Tracks 31–32. Have students read page 48 and discuss what they think the conversation is about. Explain the LANGUAGE NOTES and the PHOTO CULTURE NOTE on page 49 of the TE.

❑ *Pour communiquer:* Present the expressions and explain the two forms for "please" in the box on page 49.

❑ *Note culturelle:* Have students read *Le café* on page 49. Discuss similarities and differences in what French and American young people like to drink.

❑ *Petit commentaire:* Ask students to read the box on page 50 to find out about favorite beverages of French young people. Share the information in the TE margin. Encourage students to make comparisons to favorite American beverages.

❑ *Prononciation:* Explain French rhythm and stress patterns using the box on page 51. Guide students to accent the final syllable of a word or group of words. Use **Audio** CD 1, Track 33 to model pronunciation; have students repeat.

Guided Practice and Checking Understanding

❑ Practice expressions related to beverages with **Overhead Transparency** 11 and the Goal 1 Activity on page A61.

❑ Have students do **Workbook** Listening Activities A–E on pages 33–34 for listening practice as you play the **Audio** CD 6, Tracks 6–10 or read the **Audioscript**.

❑ Play the **Video** or read the **Videoscript** as students do **Video Activities** pages 42–44.

❑ Practice beverage vocabulary with the COMPREHENSION activity on page 49 of the TE.

Independent Practice

❑ Model the activities on pages 50–51 and have students practice on their own or in pairs. Assign Activity 3 for homework. Arrange students in pairs to practice the exchanges in Activities 1–2 and 4. Share the LANGUAGE NOTE, page 51 of the TE, if desired.

❑ Use **Communipak** *Interview* 1, page 132, *Conversations* 1–2, pages 138–140, or *Échange* 1, page 142, for additional pair practice in ordering and requesting something. Use the

**Unité 2
Leçon 3**

Lesson Plans

Discovering
FRENCH
Nouveau!

BLEU

Video Activities, page 45, for small group role plays of a scene at a café with a waiter/waitress taking customers' orders.

❑ Have students do any appropriate activities in **Activités pour tous,** pages 19–20.

Monitoring and Adjusting

❑ Have students do **Workbook** Writing Activities 1–3 on pages 36–37. Go over the answers with the class.

❑ Monitor students' language and pronunciation as they work on the activities on pages 50–51. Have them study the expressions and vocabulary in *Pour communiquer*, page 49, as needed. Use SOUNDING FRENCH on page 51 of the TE.

Reteaching

❑ Reteach portions of the lesson as needed by redoing activities from the **Activities**.

❑ Students can use the **Video** to review portions of the lesson.

Extension and Enrichment

❑ Play the GAME: C'EST LOGIQUE? on page 50 of the TE.

Summary and Closure

❑ Have students demonstrate ordering food and beverages with **Overhead Transparency** S8 and the activities on page A16. If desired, videotape the demonstrations for inclusion in students' Oral Portfolios. Guide students to summarize language expressions used for ordering food and to comment on similarities and differences between French cafés and students' favorite snack places.

LEÇON 3C Ça fait combien?, page 52

Objectives

Communicative Functions and Topics
To talk about menu items
To ask how much something costs
To ask a friend to lend you something

Linguistic Goals
To use *il* and *elle* to replace subject nouns
To pronounce the consonant "r"

Cultural Goals
To learn about the French monetary system

Motivation and Focus

❑ Ask students to look for numbers and words they know on the French money pictured on pages 52–53. Encourage students to point out the different denominations on the banknotes. Share the information in the CULTURAL NOTE, page 53 of the TE.

❑ Play **Video** 3c.3, or read the **Videoscript**. Guide students to compare French and American monetary systems.

Presentation and Explanation

❑ *Lesson Opener:* Use the WARM-UP activity on page 52 of the TE to review numbers and practice addition problems. Model and act out the conversation, using gestures and expression to clarify meaning, or play **Audio** CD 1, Tracks 34–35 or **Video** 3c.1. Ask students to read the conversation and summarize it.

❑ *Note Culturelle:* Have students read *L'argent européen* on page 52.

❑ *Pour communiquer:* Present expressions found in the box on page 53 for asking the price and asking a friend to lend money. Use the menu on **Overhead Transparency** 12 to cue questions about food prices. Point out casual speech forms in the LANGUAGE NOTE, page 53 of the TE.

❑ *Petit commentaire:* Have students read the box on page 54 to learn about types of French restaurants. Share the information in the TE margin about the **Guide Michelin**.

❑ *Prononciation:* Explain how "r" is pronounced in French using the box on page 55. Use **Audio** CD 1, Track 36 for practice.

Guided Practice and Checking Understanding

❑ Have students practice asking how much something costs with **Overhead Transparencies** 10 and 11 and the REVIEW AND PRACTICE Activities on pages A60–A61.

❑ Check students' listening comprehension with the **Audioscript** or **Audio** CD 6, Tracks 11–15 with **Workbook** Listening Activities A–E, pages 37–38.

❑ Play the **Video** or read the **Videoscript** as students do **Video Activities** pages 46–48.

Independent Practice

❑ Do the activities on pages 54–55. Activity 1 can be done for homework. Arrange students in groups of three to practice Activities 2 and 3. Have two students in each group practice the exchanges while the third student monitors their work. Students can switch roles and practice again. Have students work in pairs to prepare and present role plays for Activity 4, page 55.

❏ For pair practice with asking and answering questions about the cost of food and beverages, use **Communipak** *Tu as la parole* 1–2, *Conversation* 3, or *Tête à tête* 1 (pages 136–147). In groups of two or three, have students use page 49 of the **Video Activities** to role play customers ordering at a restaurant and asking about prices of menu items.

❏ Have students do any appropriate activities in **Activités pour tous,** pages 21–22.

Monitoring and Adjusting

❏ Have students work with **Workbook** Writing Activities 1–2, pages 39–40.

❏ Monitor students' use of the structures and expressions introduced in this lesson, as well as pronunciation. Refer them to the information in the *Pour communiquer* box on page 67 as needed. If students have difficulty pronouncing "r," use the suggestions in the PRONUNCIATION note, page 55 of the TE.

Assessment

❏ Administer Quiz 3 on pages 63–64 after the lesson's activities are completed. Use the **Test Generator** to adapt questions to your practice needs.

Reteaching

❏ Ask students to redo those activities in the **Workbook** that correspond to language items with which they are having difficulty.

❏ Students can use the **Video** to review portions of the lesson.

Extension and Enrichment

❏ Students can have extra practice with prices and menus using the GAME on page 53 of the TE. They may want to prepare their own menus as described in PROJECT, page 54 of the TE.

Summary and Closure

❏ Use the activities on page A62 of **Overhead Transparencies** with Transparency 12 to have students role play ordering in a restaurant and comparing French and American menu items. You may want to videotape selected role plays for inclusion in students' Oral Portfolios.

Discovering
FRENCH
Nouveau!

B L E U

Unité 2
Leçon 3
Block Scheduling
Lesson Plans

LEÇON 3A   Tu as faim?, page 44

Block Scheduling (1 Day to Complete)

Objectives

Communicative Functions and Topics	To say you are hungry
	To offer a friend something
	To ask a friend for something
	To talk about foods
Linguistic Goals	To use *un (sandwich)* and *une (pizza)* to understand masculine and feminine nouns
	To recognize and repeat intonation
Cultural Goals	To become aware of what kinds of fast foods French young people buy

Block Schedule

Variety When discussing French foods, bring in a variety of *crêpes* for students to try. If possible, take the class to the cafeteria or the home economics kitchen area of your school and have them prepare the *crêpes* themselves. ■

Day 1

Motivation and Focus

❑ To introduce the unit, have students look at the opener on pages 44–45. Ask them to suggest what types of food might be served at the places in the pictures. Encourage students to share prior knowledge of *cafés* and *boulangeries*. Read aloud the *Introduction culturelle*.

❑ Play **Video** 3a.3 or read the **Videoscript** for *Qu'est-ce qu'on mange?* Do the CROSS-CULTURAL OBSERVATION, page 44 of the TE.

Presentation and Explanation

❑ *Lesson Opener:* To present the opening conversations, model or play **Video** 3a.1 or **Audio** CD 1, Tracks 28–29. Then have students read the conversations; ask them to imagine what is being said. Share the information in the PHOTO CULTURE NOTE on page 45 of the TE.

❑ *Pour communiquer:* Use **Overhead Transparency** 10 to present the food names and expressions in the box on page 45.

❑ *Note culturelle:* Have students read *Les jeunes et la nourriture* on page 45. Discuss differences and similarities between what French teenagers and American teenagers eat.

❑ *Petit commentaire:* Read about French sandwiches on page 46. Share the additional information in the TE margin. Students may want to compare other American and French food items such as bread.

❑ *Grammar:* Briefly explain masculine and feminine articles and nouns in the grammar box, page 46. Revisit Transparency 10 to reinforce article and noun agreement.

❑ *Prononciation:* Point out intonation patterns in the box, page 47. Play **Audio** CD 1, Track 30 and have students repeat.

Guided Practice and Checking Understanding

❑ Practice food vocabulary with **Overhead Transparency** 10.
❑ Have students do the **Block Schedule Activity** on the previous page.
❑ Use **Block Scheduling Copymasters** 17–24.
❑ To check understanding, have students do **Workbook** Listening Activities A–E on pages 29–30 as they listen to the **Audioscript** or play **Audio** CD 6, Tracks 1–5.
❑ Play the **Video** or read the **Videoscript** and have students do pages 38–40 in the **Video Activities**.
❑ Model and reinforce students' listening skills with the COMPREHENSION activity, page 45 of the TE.

Independent Practice

❑ Have students practice ordering food with the activities on pages 46–47. Activities 2 and 4 can be completed for homework. Model Activities 1 and 3 before having students practice the dialogues in pairs.
❑ Have students work in small groups to do Activity 5 on page 41 of the **Video Activities**.
❑ Have students do any appropriate activities in **Activités pour tous,** pages 17–18.

Monitoring and Adjusting

❑ Students can do Writing Activities 1–3 on pages 31–32 of the **Workbook**.
❑ As students work on the whole-class and pair activities, monitor pronunciation and use of acticles **un** and **une**. Refer students to grammar and intonation boxes on pages 46–47. Use SOUNDING FRENCH on page 47 of the TE.

Reteaching (as needed)

❑ Help students redo any activities in the **Workbook** with which they had difficulty.
❑ Students can use the **Video** to review portions of the lesson.
❑ Reteach masculine and feminine nouns with the LISTENING PRACTICE Activity at the bottom of page 46 of the TE.

Summary and Closure

❑ Use **Overhead Transparency** S7 and the Activities on page A14 to have students demonstrate talking about foods, asking if someone is hungry, and asking for something. You may videotape the demonstrations for inclusion in students' Oral Portfolios.

Discovering
FRENCH
Nouveau!

BLEU

Unité 2
Leçon 3

Block Scheduling
Lesson Plans

LEÇON 3B Au café, page 48

Block Scheduling (1 Day to Complete)

Objectives

Communicative Functions and Topics	To identify beverages
	To say that you are thirsty
	To order a beverage in a café
	To request something from a friend and from an adult
Linguistic Goals	To use *s'il te plaît* and *s'il vous plaît*
	To stress final syllables of words or groups of words
Cultural Goals	To learn about *le café*

Block Schedule

Skit – *S'il vous plaît!* Bring props to represent the beverages taught in *Pour Communiquer* on page T63. Place the props on a table in the front of the classroom. Have students choose a partner. One student will be the server in a café and the other a customer. When you give the signal, one pair of students will race to order and serve five of the nine beverages as quickly as possible. The pair of students who accomplishes the task in the least amount of time is the winner. ■

Day 1

Motivation and Focus

❑ Ask students to look at the photos on pages 48–49; encourage them to describe the places and make comparisons to their own favorite eating places. Discuss with the class favorite beverages and places to go to get something to drink.

❑ Show the **Video** or read the **Videoscript** for section 3b.3.

Presentation and Explanation

❑ *Lesson Opener:* Do the WARM-UP AND REVIEW activity, page 48 of the TE, to review forms of address. Act out or present the opening conversations with **Video** 3b.1 or **Audio** CD 1, Tracks 31–32. Have students read page 48 and discuss what they think the conversation is about. Explain the LANGUAGE NOTES and the PHOTO CULTURE NOTE on page 48 of the TE.

❑ *Pour communiquer:* Present the expressions and explain the two forms for "please" in the box on page 49.

❑ *Note culturelle:* Have students read *Le café* on page 49. Discuss similarities and differences in what French and American young people like to drink.

❑ *Petit commentaire:* Ask students to read the box on page 50 to find out about favorite beverages of French young people. Share the information in the TE margin. Encourage students to make comparisons to favorite American beverages.

❑ *Prononciation:* Explain French rhythm and stress patterns using the box on page 51. Guide students to accent the final syllable of a word or group of words. Use **Audio** CD 1, Track 33 to model pronunciation; have students repeat.

Guided Practice and Checking Understanding

❑ Practice expressions related to beverages with **Overhead Transparency** 11 and the Goal 1 Activity on page A61.

Unité 2
Leçon 3

Block Scheduling
Lesson Plans

Discovering
FRENCH *Nouveau!*

B L E U

❑ Have students do the **Block Schedule Activity** on the previous page.
❑ Use **Block Scheduling Copymasters** 17–24.
❑ Have students do **Workbook** Listening Activities A–E on pages 33–34 for listening practice as you play the **Audio** CD 6, Tracks 6–10 or read the **Audioscript.**
❑ Play the **Video** or read the **Videoscript** as students do **Video Activities** pages 42–44.
❑ Practice beverage vocabulary with the COMPREHENSION Activity on page 49 of the TE.

Independent Practice

❑ Model the Activities on pages 50–51 and have students practice on their own or in pairs. Assign Activity 3 for homework. Arrange students in pairs to practice the exchanges in Activities 1–2 and 4. Share the LANGUAGE NOTE, page 51 of the TE, if desired.
❑ Use **Communipak** *Interview* 1, page 132, *Conversations* 1–2, pages 138–140, or *Échange* 1, page 142, for additional pair practice in ordering and requesting something. Use the **Video Activities**, page 45, for small group role plays of a scene at a café with a waiter/waitress taking customers' orders.
❑ Have students do any appropriate activities in **Activités pour tous,** pages 19–20.

Monitoring and Adjusting

❑ Have students do **Workbook** Writing Activities 1–3 on pages 36–37. Go over the answers with the class.
❑ Monitor students' language and pronunciation as they work on the Activities on pages 50–51. Have them study the expressions and vocabulary in *Pour communiquer*, page 53, as needed. Use SOUNDING FRENCH on page 51 of the TE.

Reteaching (as needed)

❑ Reteach portions of the lesson as needed by redoing activities from the **Workbook**.
❑ Students can use the **Video** to review portions of the lesson.

Extension and Enrichment (as desired)

❑ Play the GAME: C'EST LOGIQUE? on page 50 of the TE.

Summary and Closure

❑ Have students demonstrate ordering food and beverages with **Overhead Transparency** S8 and the activities on page A16. If desired, videotape the demonstrations for inclusion in students' Oral Portfolios. Guide students to summarize language expressions used for ordering food and to comment on similarities and differences between French cafés and students' favorite snack places.

Discovering
FRENCH
Nouveau!

BLEU

Unité 2
Leçon 3

Block Scheduling
Lesson Plans

LEÇON 3C Ça fait combien?, page 52

Block Scheduling (1 Day to Complete)

Objectives

Communicative Functions and Topics	To talk about menu items
	To ask how much something costs
	To ask a friend to lend you something
Linguistic Goals	To use *il* and *elle* to replace subject nouns
	To pronounce the consonant "r"
Cultural Goals	To learn about the French monetary system

Block Schedule

Change of Pace Write a café menu on the chalkboard or on a transparency. Cover the prices of the items with pieces of paper. Write the prices in scrambled order beside the menu and have students match the prices with the items on the menu. ∎

Day 1

Motivation and Focus

❑ Ask students to look for numbers and words they know on the French money pictured on pages 52–53. Encourage students to point out the different denominations on the banknotes. Share the information in the CULTURAL NOTE, page 53 of the TE.

❑ Play **Video** 3c.3, or read the **Videoscript**. Guide students to compare French and American monetary systems.

Presentation and Explanation

❑ *Lesson Opener:* Use the WARM-UP activity on page 52 of the TE to review numbers and practice addition problems. Model and act out conversation, using gestures and expressions to clarify meaning, or play **Audio** CD 1, Tracks 34–35 or **Video** 3c.1. Ask students to read the conversation and summarize it.

❑ *Note culturelle:* Have students read *L'argent européen* on page 52.

❑ *Pour communiquer:* Present expressions found in the box on page 53 for asking the price and asking a friend to lend money. Use the menu on **Overhead Transparency** 12 to cue questions about food prices. Point out casual speech forms in the LANGUAGE NOTE, page 53 of the TE.

❑ *Petit commentaire:* Have students read the box on page 54 to learn about types of French restaurants. Share the information in the TE margin about the *Guide Michelin*.

❑ *Prononciation:* Explain how "r" is pronounced in French using the box on page 55. Use **Audio** CD 1, Track 36 for practice.

Guided Practice and Checking Understanding

❑ Have students ask how much something costs with **Overhead Transparency** 10 and 11 and the REVIEW AND PRACTICE activities on page A60–A61.

❑ Have students do the **Block Schedule Activity** at the top of the page.

❑ Use **Block Scheduling Copymasters** 17–24.

❏ Check students' listening comprehension with the **Audioscript** or **Audio** CD 6, Tracks 11–15 with **Workbook** Listening Activities A–E, pages 37–38.

❏ Play the **Video** or read the **Videoscript** as students do **Video Activities** pages 46–48.

Independent Practice

❏ Do the activities on pages 54–55. Activity 1 can be done for homework. Arrange students in groups of three to practice Activities 2 and 3. Have two students in each group practice the exchanges while the third student monitors their work. Students can switch roles and practice again. Have students work in pairs to prepare and present role plays for Activity 4, page 55.

❏ For pair practice with asking and answering questions about the cost of food and beverages, use **Communipak** *Tu as la parole* 1–2, *Conversation* 3, or *Tête à tête* 1, (pages 136–147). In groups of two or three, have students use page 49 of the **Video Activities** to role play customers ordering at a restaurant and asking about prices of menu items.

❏ Have students do any appropriate activities in **Activités pour tous,** pages 21–22.

Monitoring and Adjusting

❏ Have students work with **Workbook** Writing Activities 1–2, pages 39–40.

❏ Monitor students' use of the structures and expressions introduced in this lesson, as well as pronunciation. Refer them to the information in the *Pour communiquer* box on page 67 as needed. If students have difficulty pronouncing "r," use the suggestions in the PRONUNCIATION NOTE, page 55 of the TE.

Reteaching (as needed)

❏ Ask students to redo those activities in the **Workbook** that correspond to language items with which they are having difficulty.

❏ Students can use the **Video** to review portions of the lesson.

Extension and Enrichment (as desired)

❏ Students can have extra practice with prices and menus using the GAME on page 53 of the TE. They may want to prepare their own menus as described in PROJECT, page 54 of the TE.

Summary and Closure

❏ Use the activities on page A62 of **Overhead Transparencies** with Transparency 12 to have students role play ordering in a restaurant and comparing French and American menu items. You may want to videotape selected role plays for inclusion in students' Oral Portfolios.

Assessment

❏ Administer Quiz 3 on pages 63–64 after the lesson's activities are completed. Use the **Test Generator** to adapt questions to your particular needs.

Discovering
FRENCH
Nouveau!

BLEU

Unité 2
Leçon 3

Family Letter

Date:

Dear Family,

As we continue in our exploration of French language and culture, we are learning how to get along in France. For example, we are currently learning how to order food and drink in a café, how to pay for what we order and how to use French money. In addition, we are also focusing on the basics of learning to tell time, to give the date and day of the week, and to talk about the weather.

As we move into Unit 2 of the *Discovering French, Nouveau!–Bleu* program, we continue to focus on authentic culture of France and the French-speaking world and real-life communicative situations in French. Students are deepening their understanding of the differences between their own language and French and appreciating the differences between their culture and the various cultures of the French-speaking world.

Please feel free to call me with any questions or concerns you might have as your student practices reading, writing, listening, and speaking in French.

Sincerely,

Nom _____

Classe _____ Date _____

LEÇON 3A Tu as faim?, pages 44–47

Materials Checklist

- **Student Text**
- **Audio CD 1, Tracks 28–30; CD 6, Tracks 1–5**
- **Video 1 or DVD 1; Counter 38:40–44:22**
- **Workbook**

Steps to Follow

- Unit Opener: Look at the menu in the photograph on pp. 42–43 in the text. Can you guess what **steak-frites** is? **Omelette-frites? Jus de fruits?** Are these young people ordering food at a café, a fast-food restaurant, or a street vendor? How can you tell?
- Read *Introduction culturelle* on p. 43 in the text. What is French students' favorite place to get something to eat or drink?
- Read the dialogue, *Tu as faim?*, on p. 44.
- Watch **Video** 1 or **DVD** 1; Counter 38:40–44:22, or listen to **Audio CD** 1, Tracks 28–29.
- Read *Pour communiquer* (p. 45). Write the words and expressions several times on a separate sheet of paper.
- Read *Note culturelle* (p. 45). Name one food that French students may order at a café.
- Study *Un sandwich, une pizza* on p. 46.
- Do Activity 1 in the text (p. 46). Write the parts for both speakers in complete sentences. Underline the names of foods and circle **un** or **une**.
- Do Activity 2 in the text (p. 46). Write your answers in complete sentences. Underline the names of foods and circle **un** or **une**.
- Do Activity 3 in the text (p. 47). Write the parts for both speakers on a separate sheet of paper. Check to see if you have correctly used **un** or **une**.
- Do Activity 4 in the text (p. 47). Write the answers in complete sentences on a separate sheet of paper.
- Listen to *Prononciation: l'intonation* on **Audio CD** 1, Track 30. Repeat everything you hear.
- Do **Writing Activities** 1, 2, 3 in the **Workbook** (pp. 31–32).
- Do **Listening Activities** A–E in the **Workbook** (pp. 29–30). Use **Audio CD** 6, Tracks 1–5.

If You Don't Understand . . .

- Watch the **Video** or **DVD** in a quiet place. Try to stay focused. If you get lost, stop the **Video** or **DVD**. Replay it and find your place.
- Listen to the **CDs** in a quiet place. Try to stay focused. If you get lost, stop the **CDs**. Replay them and find your place.
- Repeat aloud with the audio. Try to sound like the people on the recording.
- On a separate sheet of paper, write down the words that are new. Check for meaning.
- Say aloud anything you write. Make sure you understand everything you say.
- Write down any questions so that you can ask your partner or your teacher later.

Nom _____

Classe _____ Date _____

Discovering FRENCH *Nouveau!*

B L E U

Self-Check

What would you like to eat? Answer in complete sentences using the following expressions with **un** or **une** as appropriate.

Je voudrais . . .

1. . . . croissant
2. . . . salade
3. . . . hamburger
4. . . . hot dog
5. . . . omelette
6. . . . glace
7. . . . steak
8. . . . pizza

Answers

1. Je voudrais un croissant. 2. Je voudrais une salade. 3. Je voudrais un hamburger. 4. Je voudrais un hot dog. 5. Je voudrais une omelette. 6. Je voudrais une glace. 7. Je voudrais un steak. 8. Je voudrais une pizza.

Discovering
FRENCH
Nouveau!

BLEU

LEÇON 3B   Au café, pages 48–51

Materials Checklist

- **Student Text**
- **Audio CD 1, Tracks 31–33; CD 6, Tracks 6–10**
- **Video 1 or DVD 1; Counter 44:41–49:07**
- **Workbook**

Steps to Follow

- Read *Au café* (p. 48). Look at the pictures.
- Watch **Video** 1 or **DVD** 1; Counter 44:41–49:07, or listen to **Audio CD** 1, Tracks 31–32.
- Read *Pour communiquer* (p. 49). Write the words and expressions several times on a separate sheet of paper.
- Read *Note culturelle* (p. 49). How much is the service charge that is included in the check in French cafés?
- Do Activities 1 and 2 in the text (p. 50). On a separate sheet of paper, write the parts for both speakers. Underline the names of the drinks.
- Do Activity 3 in the text (p. 51). Write the answers in complete sentences on a separate sheet of paper.
- Do Activity 4 in the text (p. 51). On a separate sheet of paper, write the parts for both speakers in each dialogue.
- Listen to *Prononciation: l'accent final* on **Audio CD** 1, Track 33. Repeat everything you hear.
- Do **Writing Activities** 1, 2, 3 in the **Workbook** (pp. 35–36).
- Do **Listening Activities** A–E in the **Workbook** (pp. 33–34). Use **Audio CD** 6, Tracks 6–10.

If You Don't Understand . . .

- Reread activity directions. Put the directions in your own words.
- Watch the **Video** or **DVD** in a quiet place. Try to stay focused. If you get lost, stop the **Video** or **DVD**. Replay it and find your place.
- Listen to the **CDs** in a quiet place. Try to stay focused. If you get lost, stop the **CDs**. Replay them and find your place.
- Repeat aloud with the audio. Try to sound like the people on the recording.
- On a separate sheet of paper, write down the words that are new. Check for meaning.
- Write down any questions so that you can ask your partner or your teacher later.

Self-Check

Say that you would like the following foods and drinks. Underline **un** or **une**.

Je voudrais . . .

1. un / une soda
2. un / une sandwich
3. un / une café
4. un / une pizza
5. un / une glace
6. un / une limonade
7. un / une jus de tomate
8. un / une thé

Answers

1. Je voudrais un soda.   2. Je voudrais un sandwich.   3. Je voudrais un café.   4. Je voudrais une pizza.   5. Je voudrais une glace.   6. Je voudrais une limonade.   7. Je voudrais un jus de tomate.   8. Je voudrais un thé.

Nom _____

Classe _____ Date _____

Discovering
FRENCH *Nouveau!*

B L E U

Unité 2
Leçon 3

Absent Student
Copymasters

LEÇON 3C Ça fait combien?, pages 52–55

Materials Checklist
- **Student Text**
- **Audio CD** 1, Tracks 34–36; **CD** 6, Tracks 11–15
- **Video** 1 or **DVD** 1; Counter 49:38–56:29
- **Workbook**

Steps to Follow
- Read *Ça fait combien?* (p. 52).
- Watch **Video** 1 or **DVD** 1; Counter 49:38–56:29, or listen to **Audio CD** 1, Tracks 34–35.
- Read *Note culturelle* (p. 52). Which European countries use the euro?
- Read *Pour communiquer* (p. 53). Copy the new expressions.
  Copy the chart *Linking Words* (p. 53). Underline the liaisons (connected sounds) and elisions (dropped sounds).
- Do Activity 1 in the text (p. 54). Write your answers in complete sentences on a separate sheet of paper. Underline the liaisons and the elisions. Say your answers out loud.
- Do Activity 2 in the text (p. 54). Write the parts for each speaker. (Note: The price of each food item on the menu for Le Select is given on the menu.)
- Do Activity 3 in the text (p. 55). Write the parts for both speakers on a separate sheet of paper. Write out the numbers, for example, **4€30 = *Ça fait quatre euros trente.***
- Do Activity 4 in the text (p. 55). Write the parts for both speakers in complete sentences.
- Listen to *Prononciation: la consonne «r»* on **Audio CD** 1, Track 37. Repeat everything you hear.
- Do **Writing Activities** 1, 2 in the **Workbook** (pp. 39–40).
- Do **Listening Activities** A–E in the **Workbook** (pp. 37–38). Use **Audio CD** 6, Tracks 11–15.

If You Don't Understand . . .
- Reread activity directions. Put the directions in your own words.
- Write down questions so that you can ask your partner or your teacher later.
- Watch the **Video** or **DVD** in a quiet place. Try to stay focused. If you get lost, stop the **Video** or **DVD**. Replay it and find your place in the text.
- Listen to the **CDs** in a quiet place. Try to stay focused. If you get lost, stop the **CDs**. Replay them and find your place in the text.
- Listen once without repeating. Then replay and repeat aloud with the audio. Try to sound like the people on the recording. Pause the **CD** if you can't keep up.

Self-Check

Write the answers to the following questions in complete sentences on a separate sheet of paper. Provide **un** or **une**, as appropriate. Spell out the numbers.

1. . . . sandwich au jambon, ça fait combien? (5€50)
2. . . . thé, ça fait combien? (2€65)
3. . . . pizza, ça fait combien? (8€)
4. . . . glace à la vanille, ça fait combien? (2€40)
5. . . . soda, ça fait combien? (3€20)

Answers

1. Un sandwich au jambon, ça fait cinq euros cinquante. 2. Un thé, ça fait deux euros soixante-cinq. 3. Une pizza, ça fait huit euros. 4. Une glace à la vanille, ça fait deux euros quarante. 5. Un soda, ça fait trois euros vingt.

Nom _____

Classe _____ Date _____

LEÇON 3   Bon appétit!

Qu'est-ce que tu veux?

Get together with a family member. Imagine that you are both in a café. Find out what the family member wants to eat.

- First, explain your assignment.
- Next, ask the question, **Qu'est-ce que tu veux?**
- Model the pronunciation of the French words. Point to the picture as you model each answer.
- When you have an answer, complete the sentence at the bottom of the page.

un croissant

un sandwich

une crêpe

un steak-frites

une pizza

une glace

Family member: Je voudrais _____.

Nom _____

Classe _____ Date _____

Discovering
FRENCH
Nouveau!

BLEU

J'ai soif!

Get together with a family member. Imagine that the two of you are in a French café and you are thirsty. Find out what the family member wants to drink.

- First, explain your assignment.
- Next, ask the question, **Qu'est-ce que tu veux?**
- Model the pronunciation of the French words. Point to each picture as you model the pronunciation. Give any necessary English equivalents.
- When you have an answer, complete the sentence at the bottom of the page.

un jus d'orange

un thé

un jus de pomme

un chocolat

une limonade

un café

Family member: Je voudrais _____.

Discovering
FRENCH
Nouveau

BLEU

MODULE 3A Tu as faim?

Video 1, DVD 1

3a.1 Activité 1. Dialogue: Tu as faim?

Counter 38:40–39:35

What do Nathalie and Philippe want to eat? Watch the video and circle the correct response below.

1. —J'ai faim.
   Donne-moi (un sandwich / une pizza), s'il te plaît.

2. —Oh là là, oui, j'ai faim.
   Je voudrais (un hamburger / un sandwich).

3. —. . . et donne-moi aussi (une pizza / une salade).

Nom _____

Classe _____ Date _____

Discovering FRENCH *Nouveau!*

B L E U

Unité 2
Leçon 3

Video Activities

3a.2 Activité 2. Tout le monde a faim!
(Everyone is hungry!)

Counter 39:36–41:29

As people in the video say what they want to eat, put an **X** next to each food that is mentioned.

a. _____ une salade

b. _____ un sandwich jambon-gruyère

c. _____ trois croissants

d. _____ un sandwich au pâté

e. _____ une baguette

f. _____ un hot dog

g. _____ un steak-frites

h. _____ une glace à la vanille

i. _____ une glace au chocolat

j. _____ un sandwich au jambon

3a.2 Activité 3. Je voudrais . . .

As you watch the video, find out what certain people are asking for and circle the letter of the correct completion to each sentence below. The sentences are given in the order you hear them in the video.

1. Je voudrais . . .   a. *l'Express*   b. un livre

2. Je voudrais . . .   a. cet album d'Astérix   b. *l'Express*

3. Je voudrais . . .   a. un ticket de métro   b. un ticket de bus

Nom _____

Classe _____ Date _____

BLEU

 3a.3 Activité 4. Qu'est-ce qu'on mange? Counter 41:30–44:22

What snacks do French people buy at the **boulangerie**, from a street vendor, and at the café?
As you watch the **Vignette culturelle**, write the names of the snacks you can buy at the
places below.

_____   _____   _____

_____   _____   _____

_____   _____   _____

Question personnelle: What would you like to order at each of the above places?

Réponse:

_____   _____   _____

Nom _____

Classe _____ Date _____

Discovering
FRENCH
Nouveau!

BLEU

 Activité 5. Le goûter
(Snack)

Philippe is fixing sandwiches for his friends. He asks if they are hungry and which sandwich they would like. Pair up and take turns playing the role of Philippe.

> **Un sandwich . . .**
>
> **au jambon**   **au fromage**   **au pâté**   **jambon-gruyère**

▶ PHILIPPE: **Tu as faim?**
　FRIEND: **Oui, j'ai faim!**
　PHILIPPE: **Qu'est-ce que tu veux?**
　FRIEND: **Donne-moi un sandwich au fromage, s'il te plaît.**
　PHILIPPE: **Voilà.**
　FRIEND: **Merci!**

Nom _____

Classe _____ Date _____

B L E U

MODULE 3B Au café

 3b.1 Activité 1. Dialogue: Au café

Counter 44:41–45:38

Who is asking the questions below? Watch
the video and mark an **X** under the
appropriate photo.

1. Tu as soif?   ❑   ❑

2. On va dans un café?   ❑   ❑

3. Vous désirez, mademoiselle?   ❑   ❑

4. Et vous, monsieur?   ❑   ❑

5. La limonade, c'est pour vous, mademoiselle?   ❑   ❑

Nom _____

Classe _____ Date _____

3b.2 Activité 2. S'il vous plaît

Counter 45:39–47:27

Watch as the people in the video ask for the following things. Place a check mark under the appropriate picture each time that item is mentioned.

a. _____

b. _____

c. _____

d. _____

e. _____

f. _____

g. _____

h. _____

i. _____

j. _____

Nom _____

Classe _____ Date _____

 3b.3 Activité 3. La carte des boissons
(The beverage menu)

Counter 47:28–49:07

A. What are some typical French beverages? As you watch the **Vignette culturelle**, write a brief description (in English) of each drink in the beverage menu below.

LA CARTE DES BOISSONS

Jus de Fruit

un citron pressé _____

une orange pressée _____

Sodas

une limonade _____

un diabolo-menthe _____

un diabolo-fraise _____

B. Now it's your turn to order! Choose a beverage from the menu above and answer the following question.

Question personnelle: Qu'est-ce que vous désirez?

Réponse: Je voudrais_____

Discovering FRENCH *Nouveau!*

B L E U

Activité 4. Vous désirez?

In groups of 3 or 4, act out a scene using what you have learned about taking and placing orders in a café. One student plays the role of the waiter or waitress and the others play customers in the café. Each customer orders a drink from the menu in **Activité 3**. Take turns playing the part of the waiter or waitress.

▶ CUSTOMER 1: **Monsieur, s'il vous plaît!**
WAITER: **Vous désirez, mademoiselle?**
CUSTOMER 1: **Un citron pressé, s'il vous plaît!**
WAITER: **Et pour vous, monsieur?**
CUSTOMER 2: **Donnez-moi un diabolo-fraise, s'il vous plaît.**
WAITER: **Mais oui, monsieur.**

Nom _____

Classe _____ Date _____

MODULE 3C Ça fait combien?

3c.1 Activité 1. Dialogue: Ça fait combien?

Counter 49:38–50:15

How much does Trinh's check come to?
Listen to the video and then fill in the prices
and the total amount in the bill below.

LE SELECT

1 JUS D'ORANGE   _____ €

1 LIMONADE   _____ €

            TOTAL   _____ €

SERVICE COMPRIS
MERCI

3c.2 Activité 2. Ça fait combien?

Counter 50:16–52:15

How many euros do the people in the video have to pay? In each item below, circle the letter
of the correct amount.

1. a. 5 euros 40   b. 5 euros 50

2. a. 4 euros   b. 14 euros

3. a. 6 euros 20   b. 16 euros

4. a. 3 euros 72   b. 3 euros 52

5. a. 2 euros   b. 12 euros

6. a. 15 euros   b. 5 euros

7. a. 59 euros   b. 49 euros

Nom _____

Classe _____ Date _____

Discovering
FRENCH
Nouveau!

B L E U

Unité 2
Leçon 3

Video Activities

3c.3 Activité 3. L'argent français

As you watch the **Vignette culturelle**, decide whether each statement below
is true (**vrai**) or false (**faux**). Mark an **X** in the appropriate column.

	vrai	faux
1. When you travel in a foreign country, you need to have U.S. dollars to pay for things you want to buy.	❑	❑
2. In France, the type of money you will need is called the **euro.**	❑	❑
3. The French people have been using **l'euro** since January, 2000.	❑	❑
4. Before the **euro,** the French were using a different currency called the dollar.	❑	❑
5. The **euro** is also used in most European countries.	❑	❑
6. The Germans, the Italians, the Spanish, and the Dutch also use the **euro.**	❑	❑
7. The **euro** is also the currency of Québec in Canada.	❑	❑

3c.3 Activité 4. Les billets *(Bills)*

As you watch the **Vignette culturelle**, Nicole will explain the different euro bills. Draw a line from the picture of the euro bill on the left to its corresponding color on the right.

1.    Il est vert.

2.    Il est orange.

3.    Il est rouge.

4.    Il est jaune.

5.    Il est violet.

6.    Il est bleu.

7.    Il est gris.

Nom _____

Classe _____ Date _____

Discovering
FRENCH *Nouveau!*

B L E U

Unité 2
Leçon 3

Video Activities

 Activité 5. Au Restaurant Le Select

Form a group with two or three classmates. One student plays the role of a waiter or waitress, the others play friends eating at a restaurant. Act out a scene using what you have learned about ordering in a restaurant and asking how much things cost. Switch roles so everyone in your group has a chance to be the waiter or waitress. Some useful sentences are listed below to help you with your scene.

《》

Phrases utiles
Monsieur (Mademoiselle), s'il vous plaît.
Vous désirez?
Je voudrais . . .
Donnez-moi . . .
Ça fait combien, s'il vous plaît?
Ça fait . . .

LE SELECT
CAFÉ RESTAURANT

BOISSONS

café ....1€50
chocolat ....2€50
thé ....2€
limonade ....2€50
jus d'orange ....2€70
jus de raisin ....2€70

GLACES

glace au chocolat ....2€50
glace à la vanille ....2€50

SANDWICHS

sandwich au jambon .....3€50
sandwich au fromage ....3€50

ET AUSSI . . .

steak-frites ....8€
salade mixte ....3€50
salade de tomates ....4€
omelette ....4€25
hot dog ....4€
croissant ....1€40
pizza ....8€

MODULE 3A Tu as faim?

Video 1, DVD 1

After school, Pierre and his friends Philippe and Nathalie like to have a snack before going home. Often they stop to buy sandwiches and pizza! Today it's Pierre's turn to treat his friends.

3a.1 Dialogue: Tu as faim?

Counter 38:40–39:35

PIERRE: Tu as faim?
NATHALIE: Oui, j'ai faim.
PIERRE: Qu'est-ce que tu veux, un sandwich ou une pizza?
NATHALIE: Donne-moi une pizza, s'il te plaît.
PIERRE: Voilà.
NATHALIE: Merci.
PIERRE: Et toi, Philippe, tu as faim?
PHILIPPE: Oh là, là, oui, j'ai faim.
PIERRE: Qu'est-ce que tu veux, un sandwich ou une pizza?
PHILIPPE: Je voudrais un sandwich . . . euh . . . et donne-moi aussi une pizza.
PIERRE: C'est vrai! Tu as vraiment faim!

3a.2 Mini-scenes: Ordering food

Counter 39:36–41:29

*Did you notice how Philippe told Pierre what he would like? He says **je voudrais**. "I would like." Watch again.*

PHILIPPE: Je voudrais un sandwich.

Now watch people order various types of food.

—Mademoiselle?
—Je voudrais un hot dog.
—Voici.
—Merci.

—Je voudrais trois croissants, s'il vous plaît.
—Oui . . . Voici.

—Je voudrais une glace à la vanille.
—Voici.
—Merci.

—Je voudrais un steak-frites . . .
—Oui.
—. . . et une salade.
—D'accord.

—Je voudrais un sandwich au jambon.
—Et moi, je voudrais un sandwich au pâté.

***Je voudrais** is used to ask for all types of things. Watch how these people ask for a magazine, a book, and a subway ticket.*

—Je voudrais *l'Express.*
—Voici.

—Je voudrais cet album d'Astérix.

—Je voudrais un ticket de métro.
—Voilà.
—Merci.

Now it's your turn. You're in a café in France. Ask for the following things.

[screen card]
—Je voudrais un sandwich.

[screen card]
—Je voudrais une salade.

[screen card]
—Je voudrais un croissant.

[screen card]
—Je voudrais un steak-frites.

3a.3 Vignette culturelle: Qu'est-ce qu'on mange?

Counter 41:30–44:22

*Do you ever feel hungry during the course of the day? In France, there are many places where you can have something to eat. For example, you can stop at a **boulangerie**. French **boulangeries** sell various kinds of bread. They also sell croissants and other types of pastries.*

You can ask for:

> **un éclair**
> **un pain au chocolat**
> **un pain aux raisins et**
> **une brioche . . .**

You can also stop at a street vendor. Here you can buy pizza.

*Here you can order **crêpes**.*

Here you can have a hot dog or **une saucisse**.

You can also sit down at a café. The most common type of snack that young people have in a café is a sandwich. There is always a large selection of sandwiches that you can choose from. For example:

un sandwich au jambon
This is a ham sandwich.
un sandwich au fromage
This a cheese sandwich.
un sandwich au pâté
This is a sandwich made with pâté, a delicious meat spread.

In this café, you can also order **un sandwich jambon-gruyère**, which is made with ham and Swiss cheese.

Let's ask these young people what they're eating. **Qu'est-ce que vous mangez?** What are you eating?

Qu'est-ce que vous mangez?

—Je mange un sandwich au pâté.
—Je mange un sandwich au fromage.
—Je mange un sandwich au jambon.

As you can see, French sandwiches do not look like American sandwiches. First, they are made with a typical French bread called **une baguette**. Outside it has a tasty golden crust. Inside the bread is soft. To make a sandwich, you cut a section of baguette in half and spread a thin layer of butter and then add cheese, ham, or pâté, as you wish. This sandwich is being made with a delicious ham called **jambon de Paris**. Now your sandwich is ready to be served.

—Voici votre sandwich. Bon appétit!

Unité 2
Leçon 3

Videoscripts

Discovering
FRENCH
Nouveau!

BLEU

MODULE 3B Au café

Video 1, DVD 1

This afternoon, Trinh and Céline went shopping. They are now tired and thirsty. Trinh invites Céline to a café.

3b.1 Dialogue: Au café

Counter 44:41–45:38

TRINH:	Tu as soif?
CÉLINE:	Oui, j'ai soif.
TRINH:	On va dans un café? Je t'invite.
CÉLINE:	D'accord!
LE GARÇON:	Vous désirez, mademoiselle?
CÉLINE:	Un jus d'orange, s'il vous plaît.
LE GARÇON:	Et vous, monsieur?
TRINH:	Donnez-moi une limonade, s'il vous plaît.
LE GARÇON:	La limonade, c'est pour vous, mademoiselle?
TRINH:	Non, c'est pour moi.
LE GARÇON:	Ah, excusez-moi. Voici le jus d'orange, mademoiselle.
CÉLINE:	Merci.

3b.2 Mini-scenes: Saying please

Counter 45:39–47:27

Did you notice how Trinh and Céline said "please" when they ordered a drink? Watch again.

LE GARÇON:	Vous désirez, mademoiselle?
CÉLINE:	Un jus d'orange, s'il vous plaît.
LE GARÇON:	Et vous, monsieur?
TRINH:	Donnez-moi une limonade, s'il vous plaît.

To say "please" formally, the French use the expression **s'il vous plaît**. *Watch.*

—Une limonade, s'il vous plaît.
—Je voudrais un jus de pomme, s'il vous plaît.
—Un café, s'il vous plaît.
—Donnez-moi un chocolat, s'il vous plaît.
—Je voudrais trois croissants, s'il vous plaît.
—Je voudrais *l'Express*, s'il vous plaît.
—Je voudrais un ticket de métro, s'il vous plaît.

To say "please" to a friend or a member of their family, French teenagers say **s'il te plaît**.

—Donne-moi un soda, s'il te plaît.
—Donne-moi un jus de raisin, s'il te plaît.
—Donne-moi *l'Express*, s'il te plaît.

Now it's your turn. Imagine you're in a French café. The waiter comes to take your order. Tell him you would like the items you see pictured. Be sure to use the polite form of "please," **s'il vous plaît**.

—Vous désirez?   [screen card]
—Je voudrais un thé, s'il vous plaît.

—Vous désirez?   [screen card]
—Je voudrais un jus d'orange, s'il vous plaît.

—Vous désirez?   [screen card]
—Je voudrais un croissant, s'il vous plaît.

—Vous désirez?   [screen card]
—Je voudrais un steak-frites, s'il vous plaît.

3b.3 Vignette culturelle: Qu'est-ce qu'on boit?
Counter 47:28–49:07

If you were going to a French café, what would you order to drink? Let's see what French teenagers drink.

Mineral water is very popular. French people drink it at home with meals, and they also order it in cafés.

French teenagers also drink lots of fruit juices. Let's ask these girls what kind of juice they're drinking.

Qu'est-ce que vous buvez?

—Je bois un jus d'orange.
—Moi, je bois un jus de pomme.
—Et moi, je bois un jus de tomate.
—Moi, je bois un citron pressé.

Un citron pressé *is a very refreshing summer drink. It's real lemonade. The*

waiter brings you freshly squeezed lemon juice mixed with sugar, and you add the water. In French cafés you can also order **une orange pressée**. *Can you guess what* **une orange pressée** *is?*

You can also order all sorts of carbonated drinks. **Diabolos** *are popular drinks made with* **limonade**.

Qu'est-ce que c'est que ça?
—C'est un diabolo-menthe.
Et ça, qu'est-ce que c'est?
—C'est un diabolo-fraise.

Limonade *is a carbonated drink with a slight lemon flavor. It's mixed with natural concentrated syrups.* **Un diabolo-menthe** *is* **limonade** *with mint syrup.* **Un diabolo-fraise** *is* **limonade** *with strawberry syrup.*

Cafés always have lots of drinks to choose from. In France everyone likes to sit, order something to drink, and watch the people go by.

MODULE 3C Ça fait combien?

Video 1, DVD 1

At the café, Trinh and Céline have talked about many things. Now it's time to go, and Trinh wants to pay the bill. He calls the waiter.

3c.1 Dialogue: Ça fait combien?

Counter 49:38–50:15

TRINH: S'il vous plaît?

LE GARÇON: Oui, monsieur.

TRINH: Ça fait combien?

LE GARÇON: Voyons, un jus d'orange, 2 € 50, et une limonade, 1 € 50. Ça fait 4 €.

TRINH: 4 € . . . Très bien . . . Zut! Où est mon porte-monnaie . . .? Dis, Céline, prête-moi 5 €, s'il te plaît.

3c.2 Mini-scenes:
Asking what one owes Counter 50:16–52:15

Did you notice what Trinh said to ask the waiter how much he owed him? Watch again.

LE GARÇON: Oui, monsieur.

TRINH: Ça fait combien?

LE GARÇON: Voyons, un jus d'orange, 2 € 50, et une limonade, 1 € 50. Ça fait 4 €.

TRINH: 4 € . . .

To ask how much you owe, you can say:
Ça fait combien? *or* **C'est combien?**
Let's watch.

—C'est combien?
—5 euros 50.

—Ça fait combien?
—4 euros, s'il vous plaît.

—C'est combien, s'il vous plaît?
—6 euros 20.
—Voici.
—Merci.

—Bonjour.
—Bonjour.
—Je voudrais 4 pains au chocolat, s'il vous plaît.
—Voici.
—Ça fait combien, s'il vous plaît?
—Alors, ça fait 3 euros 52 s'il vous plaît.

—Merci.
—Merci.
—Au revoir.
—Au revoir.

—C'est combien monsieur?
—2 euros, s'il vous plaît . . . Merci . . . Au revoir.
—Au revoir.

—C'est combien?
—C'est 15 euros, mademoiselle.
—Merci.

—C'est combien?
—49 euros, monsieur.

Now imagine that you're in a French café with friends. You've ordered sandwiches, which cost 3 euros each, and soft drinks, which cost 2 euros each. Someone will want to know how much your order costs. Give an answer.

—Ça fait combien?   [screen card]
—Ça fait 6 euros.

—Ça fait combien?   [screen card]
—Ça fait 5 euros.

—Ça fait combien?   [screen card]
—Ça fait 8 euros.

—Ça fait combien?   [screen card]
—Ça fait 10 euros.

3c.3 Vignette culturelle: L'argent français Counter 52:16–56:29

When you travel in a foreign country, you need to have the currency of that country to pay for the things you want to buy.

*In France, you will need euros or as the French say, "**euros**."*

*The French people have been using the euro, "**l'euro**," since January 2002.*

Before, they were using a different currency called the franc, *"le franc."*

The euro is a very handy currency to have when you travel in Europe because it is used not only in France but in most European countries.

The Germans, the Italians, the Spanish, the Portuguese, the Dutch, the Irish, the Greeks . . . All these people also use the euro.

Now let's look at this modern European currency.

This is a five euro bill.

On the right, you can see a map of Europe, with France here.

On the left, you see a bridge. This bridge symbolizes the economic union between the different countries that use the euro.

As you can see, the various euro bills are of different colors, and also of different sizes.

This is the largest euro bill. It is worth 500 euros. It is purple.
Voici le billet de 500 euros. Il est violet.

This is the 200 euro bill. It is yellow.
Voici le billet de 200 euros. Il est jaune.

This is the 100 euro bill. It is green.
Voici le billet de 100 euros. Il est vert.

This is the 50 euro bill. It is orange.
Voici le billet de 50 euros. Il est orange.

This is the 20 euro bill. It is blue.
Voici le billet de 20 euros. Il est bleu.

This is the ten euro bill. It is red.
Voici le billet de 10 euros. Il est rouge.

And finally the smallest bill is worth 5 euros. It is gray.
Voici le billet de 5 euros. Il est gris.

There are also 8 different coins: des pièces.

Voici la pièce d'un euro, et voici la pièce de deux euros.

Voici la pièce d'un centime . . .
la pièce de deux centimes . . .
la pièce de cinq centimes . . .
la pièce de dix centimes . . .
la pièce de vingt centimes . . .
et la pièce de cinquante centimes.

Now you know all about French money.

Before we leave, we will help you learn how to count money in French.

Listen and repeat. **Écoutez et répétez.**

un euro
un euro

deux euros
deux euros

trois euros
trois euros

quatre euros
quatre euros

cinq euros
cinq euros

six euros
six euros

sept euros
sept euros

huit euros
huit euros

neuf euros
neuf euros

dix euros
dix euros

Now, when you go to Paris, you will have no problems buying things.

LEÇON 3   Bon appétit!

PE AUDIO

Vidéo-scène A. Tu as faim?

CD 1, Track 28

Compréhension orale
Listening Comprehension, p. 44

Pierre, Philippe, and Nathalie are on their way home from school. They stop by a street vendor who sells sandwiches and pizza. Today it is Pierre's turn to treat his friends.

Scène 1. Pierre et Nathalie

PIERRE: Tu as faim?
NATHALIE: Oui, j'ai faim.
PIERRE: Tu veux, un sandwich ou une pizza?
NATHALIE: Donne-moi une pizza, s'il te plaît.
PIERRE: Voilà.
NATHALIE: Merci.

Scène 2. Pierre et Philippe

PIERRE: Et toi, Philippe, tu as faim?
PHILIPPE: Oh là, là, oui, j'ai faim.
PIERRE: Qu'est-ce que tu veux, un sandwich ou une pizza?
PHILIPPE: Je voudrais un sandwich . . . euh . . . et donne-moi aussi une pizza.
PIERRE: C'est vrai! Tu as vraiment faim!

CD 1, Track 29

Écoutez et répétez. Listen and repeat. p. 44

You will now hear a paused version of the dialog. Listen to the speaker and repeat right after he or she has completed the sentence.

Prononciation

CD 1, Track 30

L'intonation, p. 47

Écoutez: Voici un steak . . . et une salade.

When you speak, your voice rises and falls. This is called INTONATION. In French, as in English, your voice goes down at the end of a statement. However, in French, your voice rises after each group of words in the middle of a sentence. (This is the opposite of English, where your voice drops a little when you pause in the middle of a sentence.)

Répétez: Je voudrais une pizza. #
Je voudrais une pizza et un sandwich. #
Je voudrais une pizza, un sandwich et un hamburger. #
Voici un steak. #
Voici un steak et une salade. #
Voici un steak, une salade et une glace. #

Vidéo-scène B. Au café

CD 1, Track 31

Compréhension orale
Listening Comprehension, p. 48

This afternoon Trinh and Céline went shopping. They are now tired and thirsty. Trinh invites Céline to a café.

Scène 1

TRINH: Tu as soif?
CÉLINE: Oui, j'ai soif.
TRINH: On va dans un café? Je t'invite.
CÉLINE : D'accord!

Scène 2.

LE GARÇON: Vous désirez, mademoiselle?
CÉLINE: Un jus d'orange, s'il vous plaît.
LE GARÇON: Et pour vous, monsieur?
TRINH: Donnez-moi une limonade, s'il vous plaît.

Scène 3.

Le garçon: La limonade, c'est pour vous, mademoiselle?

TRINH: Non, c'est pour moi.
LE GARÇON: Ah, excusez-moi. Voici le jus d'orange, mademoiselle.
CÉLINE: Merci.

CD 1, Track 32

Écoutez et répétez. Listen and repeat. p. 48

You will now hear a paused version of the dialogue. Listen to the speaker and repeat right after he or she has completed the sentence.

Prononciation

CD 1, Track 33

L'accent final, p. 51

Écoutez: un chocolat

In French, the rhythm is very even and the accent always falls on the *last* syllable of a word or group of words.

Répétez: Philippe # Thomas # Alice # Sophie # Dominique # un café # Je voudrais un café. # une salade # Donnez-moi une salade. # un chocolat # Donne-moi un chocolat. #

Vidéo-scène C. Ça fait combien?

CD 1, Track 34

Compréhension orale
Listening Comprehension, p. 52

At the café, Trinh and Céline have talked about many things. It is now time to go.

Trinh calls the waiter so he can pay the check.

TRINH: S'il vous plaît?
LE GARÇON: Oui, monsieur.
TRINH: Ça fait combien?
LE GARÇON: Voyons, un jus d'orange, 2 euros 50, et une limonade, 1 euro 50. Ça fait 4 euros.
TRINH: 4 euros . . . Très bien . . . Mais, euh . . . Zut! Où est mon porte-monnaie . . .? Dis, Céline, prête-moi 5 euros, s'il te plaît.

CD 1, Track 35

Écoutez et répétez. Listen and repeat. p. 52

You will now hear a paused version of the dialogue. Listen to the speaker and repeat right after he or she has completed the sentence.

Prononciation

CD 1, Track 36

La consonne "r," p. 55

Écoutez: Marie

The French consonant "r" is not at all like the English "r". It is pronounced at the back of the throat. In fact, it is similar to the Spanish "jota" sound of José.

Répétez: Marie # Paris # orange # Henri # franc # très # croissant # fromage # bonjour # pour # Pierre # quart # Robert # Richard # Renée # Raoul # Marie, prête-moi trente euros. #

....

WORKBOOK AUDIO

Vidéo-scène A. Tu as faim?

Section 1. Au café

CD 6, Track 1

A. Compréhension orale
Listening Comprehension, p. 29

You will hear several people saying what they would like to eat. Each dialogue has a number. In your Workbook, find the item that the person is asking for and write the corresponding dialogue number in the space provided. The first dialogue is a model.

Modèle: 1. Je voudrais un sandwich.

You would write "1" under "d": un sandwich.
  2. —Mademoiselle?
    —Je voudrais un hot dog.
    —Voici.
    —Merci. #

3. —Je voudrais trois croissants, s'il vous plaît.
   —Oui . . . Voici. #

4. —Je voudrais une glace à la vanille.
   —Voici.
   —Merci. #

5. —Je voudrais un steak-frites . . .
   —Oui.
   —. . . et une salade.
   —D'accord. #

6. —Je voudrais un sandwich au jambon.
   —Et moi, je voudrais un sandwich au pâté. #

Now check your answers. You should have matched the pictures with the conversations as follows: a-3, b-4, c-2, d-1, e-6, and f-5.

CD 6, Track 2

B. Écoutez et répétez.
Listen and repeat. p. 29

Listen and repeat the names of the various foods you see in your Workbook. Note that the foods in the top row are masculine and are introduced by "un." The foods in the bottom row are feminine and are introduced by "une." Repeat the name of each food twice.

Commençons. Let's begin.
1. un croissant # un croissant #
2. un sandwich # un sandwich #
3. un steak # un steak #
4. un steak-frites # un steak-frites #
5. un hamburger # un hamburger #
6. un hot dog # un hot dog #
7. une salade # une salade #
8. une pizza # une pizza #
9. une omelette # une omelette #
10. une crêpe # une crêpe #
11. une glace # une glace #

CD 6, Track 3

C. Questions et réponses
Questions and answers, p. 30

Now it's your turn to ask for things. You are in a café. Listen as the speaker on the recording asks you which of two things you would like. Say that you want the item in the picture, using **je voudrais.** Then listen for the confirmation. Here is a model.

Modèle: Tu veux un sandwich ou une pizza? *(response)* Je voudrais un sandwich.

1. Tu veux un sandwich ou une pizza? #
   Je voudrais une pizza.

2. Tu veux une omelette ou une salade? #
   Je voudrais une salade.

3. Tu veux un steak ou un hamburger? #
   Je voudrais un hamburger.

4. Tu veux un croissant ou une crêpe? #
   Je voudrais un croissant.

5. Tu veux un steak-frites ou un hot dog? #
   Je voudrais un steak-frites.

Section 2. Intonation

CD 6, Track 4

D. Écoutez et répétez.
Listen and repeat. p. 30

When you speak, your voice rises and falls. This is called "intonation." In French, as in English, your voice goes down at the end of a statement. However, in French, your voice rises after each group of words in the middle of a sentence. Listen:

Voici un steak . . . et une salade.

This is the opposite of English, where your voice drops a little whenever you pause in the middle of a sentence.

Listen and repeat the French sentences in your Workbook, imitating the intonation of the speaker.

Je voudrais une pizza. #

Je voudrais une pizza et un sandwich. #

Je voudrais une pizza, un sandwich et un hamburger. #

Voici un steak. #

Voici un steak et une salade. #

Voici un steak, une salade et une glace. #

Section 3. Dictée

CD 6, Track 5

E. Écoutez et écrivez.
Listen and write. p. 30

You will hear a short dialogue spoken twice. First listen carefully to what the people are saying. The second time you hear the dialogue, fill in the missing words.

Écoutez.

—Oh là là! J'ai faim!
—Qu'est-ce que tu veux? Un steak ou une pizza?
—Donne-moi un steak, s'il te plaît.

Listen again and fill in the missing words.

Vidéo-scène B. Au café

Section 1. Au café

CD 6, Track 6

A. Écoutez et répétez.
Listen and repeat. p. 33

Listen and repeat the names of the various beverages you see in your Workbook. Be careful to distinguish between **un** and **une**. Repeat the name of each beverage twice.

Commençons. Let's begin.

1. un soda # un soda #
2. un jus d'orange # un jus d'orange #
3. un jus de pomme # un jus de pomme #
4. un jus de tomate # un jus de tomate #
5. un jus de raisin # un jus de raisin #
6. une limonade # une limonade
7. un café # un café #
8. un thé # un thé #
9. un chocolat # un chocolat #

Section 2. S'il te plaît, donne-moi . . .

CD 6, Track 7

B. Questions et réponses
Questions and answers, p. 33

Imagine you are at a friend's house and are being offered something to drink. Ask your friend to please give you the item in the picture. Then listen for the confirmation.

Modèle: Tu veux un café ou un thé?
(response) S'il te plaît, donne-moi un café.

1. Tu veux un soda ou un thé? #
S'il te plaît, donne-moi un soda.

2. Tu veux un jus de tomate ou un jus d'orange? #
S'il te plaît, donne-moi un jus de tomate.

3. Tu veux un jus de raisin ou un jus de pomme? #
S'il te plaît, donne-moi un jus de pomme.

4. Tu veux un chocolat ou un café? #
S'il te plaît, donne-moi un chocolat.

Section 3. Je voudrais …

CD 6, Track 8

C. Questions et réponses
Questions and answers, p. 34

Imagine you are in a French café. When the waiter asks you what you would like, order the item in the picture, using **je voudrais** and the polite form of *please*, **s'il vous plaît.** Listen for the confirmation.

Modèle: Vous désirez?
(response) Je voudrais un thé, s'il vous plaît.

1. Vous désirez? #
Je voudrais un jus d'orange, s'il vous plaît.

2. Vou désirez? #
Je voudrais un croissant, s'il vous plaît.

BLEU

3. Vous désirez? #
   Je voudrais un steak-frites, s'il vous plaît.

4. Vous désirez? #
   Je voudrais une omelette, s'il vous plaît.

Section 4. Conversations

CD 6, Track 9

D. Compréhension orale
Listening comprehension, p. 34

You will hear a series of short conversations between different people. Listen to each conversation carefully. Then answer the corresponding questions in your Workbook by circling the appropriate letter (a, b, or c). You will hear each conversation twice.

Commençons. Let's begin.

1. —Tu as soif?
   —Oui, donne-moi une limonade, s'il te plaît.

Listen again.

2. —Tu veux un jus d'orange?
   —Non, merci. Donne-moi un jus de raisin, s'il te plaît.

Listen again.

3. —Vous désirez, mademoiselle?
   —Je voudrais une glace, s'il vous plaît.

Listen again.

4. —Tu as soif?
   —Non, j'ai faim.
   —Qu'est-ce que tu veux?
   —Donne-moi un hot dog, s'il te plaît.

Listen again.

Now check your answers. You should have circled 1-b, 2-c, 3-a, and 4-c.

Section 5. Dictée

CD 6, Track 10

E. Écoutez et écrivez.
Listen and write. p. 34

You will hear a short dialogue spoken twice. First listen carefully to what the people are saying. The second time you hear the dialogue, fill in the missing words.

Écoutez.

—Vous désirez, mademoiselle?
—Je voudrais un chocolat.
—Et vous, monsieur?
—Donnez-moi un thé, s'il vous plaît.

Listen again and fill in the missing words.

Vidéo-scène C. Ça fait combien?

Section 1. L'euro

CD 6, Track 11

A. Écoutez et répétez.
Listen and repeat. p. 37

When you go to France, you will make your purchases in euros. Repeat the following sums after the speaker. Repeat each amount twice.

Commençons. Let's begin.

un euro # un euro #

deux euros # deux euros #

trois euros # trois euros #

quatre euros # quatre euros #

cinq euros # cinq euros #

six euros # six euros #

sept euros # sept euros #

huit euros # huit euros #

neuf euros # neuf euros #

dix euros # dix euros #

Discovering
FRENCH *Nouveau!*

BLEU

Unité 2
Leçon 3

Audioscripts

Section 2. C'est combien?

CD 6, Track 12

B. Compréhension orale
Listening Comprehension, p. 37

In the following dialogues, people are asking for prices. Listen carefully and write the amount you hear in the appropriate box in your Workbook.

Listen to the model.

Modèle: —Ça fait combien?
—Dix euros, s'il vous plaît.

You would write ten euros.

Commençons. Let's begin.

1. —C'est combien?
   —Six euros. #

2. —C'est combien, s'il vous plaît?
   —Huit euros.
   —Voici.
   —Merci. #

3. —Voici.
   —Ça fait combien, s'il vous plaît?
   —Ça fait dix-neuf euros. #

4. —C'est combien?
   —Vingt-deux euros, s'il vous plaît. #

5. —C'est combien?
   —Trente-cinq euros, monsieur.
   —D'accord. #

Now check your answers.

Number 1. Six euros.
Number 2. Eight euros.
Number 3. Nineteen euros.
Number 4. Twenty-two euros.
Number 5. Thirty-five euros.

CD 6, Track 13

C. Questions et réponses
Questions and answers, p. 37

Imagine you are in a French café. Look at the prices. Sandwiches cost 3 euros and soft drinks cost 2 euros. Someone will ask you what each order costs. Answer her. You will

hear a confirmation so that you can check if you have given the right answer.

1. Ça fait combien? # Ça fait 6 euros.
2. Ça fait combien? # Ça fait 5 euros.
3. Ça fait combien? # Ça fait 8 euros.
4. Ça fait combien? # Ça fait 10 euros.

Section 3. Conversations

CD 6, Track 14

D. Compréhension orale
Listening comprehension, p. 38

You will hear a series of short conversations between different people. Listen to each conversation carefully. Then answer the corresponding questions in your Workbook by circling the appropriate letter (a, b, or c). You will hear each conversation twice.

Commençons. Let's begin.

1. —Combien coûte la pizza?
   —Elle coûte sept euros.

Listen again.

2. —Ça fait combien, s'il vous plaît?
   —Ça fait treize euros, mademoiselle.

Listen again.

3. —Christine?
   —Oui? Qu'est-ce que tu veux?
   —Prête-moi dix euros, s'il te plaît.

Listen again.

Now check your answers. You should have circled 1-b, 2-a, and 3-b.

Section 4. Dictée

CD 6, Track 15

E. Écoutez et écrivez.
Listen and write. p. 38

You will hear a short dialogue spoken twice. First listen carefully to what the people are saying. The second time you hear the dialogue, fill in the missing words.

Écoutez.
—Combien coûte l'omelette?
—Elle coûte trois euros cinquante.
—Et la glace?
—Deux euros cinquante.

—Ça fait six euros au total.
Dis, Mélanie, prête-moi six euros, s'il te plaît.

Listen again and fill in the missing words.

LESSON 3 QUIZ

Part I: Listening

CD 13, Track 12

A. Conversations

You will hear a series of short conversations between various French teenagers. Listen to each conversation carefully. Then answer the corresponding questions on your answer sheet by circling the appropriate letter (a, b, or c). You will hear each conversation twice.

Let's begin.

1. FILLE: Qu'est-ce que tu veux?
   GARÇON: Je voudrais une glace, s'il te plaît.

2. GARÇON: Tu veux un steak?
   FILLE: Non, merci. Je suis végétarienne.
   GARÇON: Qu'est-ce que tu veux alors?
   FILLE: Une pizza, s'il te plaît.

3. GARÇON: Tu veux un jus d'orange?
   FILLE: Non, merci. Donne-moi un jus de pomme, s'il te plaît.

4. FILLE: Tu as soif?
   GARÇON: Non, j'ai faim.
   FILLE: Qu'est-ce que tu veux?
   GARÇON: Donne-moi un hamburger, s'il te plaît.

5. FEMME: C'est combien, s'il vous plaît?
   HOMME: Ça fait 2 euros pour le café et 1 euro pour le croissant.

Nom _____

Classe _____ Date _____

Discovering
FRENCH *Nouveau!*

B·L·E·U

Unité 2
Leçon 3 Lesson Quiz

QUIZ 3

Part I: Listening

A. Conversations (30 points)

You will hear a series of short conversations between various French teenagers. Listen to each conversation carefully. Then answer the corresponding questions on your answer sheet by circling the appropriate letter (a, b, or c). You will hear each conversation twice.

1. What would the boy like to have?
   a. a croissant
   b. an omelet
   c. an ice cream

2. What type of food does the girl NOT eat?
   a. meat
   b. Italian food
   c. vegetables

3. What would the girl like to drink?
   a. a glass of orange juice
   b. a glass of apple juice
   c. a glass of grape juice

4. How does the boy feel?
   a. tired
   b. hungry
   c. thirsty

5. What did the lady order?
   a. only something to eat
   b. only something to drink
   c. something to eat and something to drink

Nom _____

Classe _____ Date _____

Discovering
FRENCH
Nouveau!

B L E U

Part II: Writing

B. En France (30 points)

List three foods and three beverages that you can order in a French café or fast-food place. Make sure to use **un** or **une**, as appropriate.

1. _____

2. _____

3. _____

4. _____

5. _____

6. _____

C. Expression personnelle (30 points)

You are in a French café.

- Tell the waitress that you are thirsty.

  _____

- Ask her politely to give you something to drink. (Choose the beverage you want.)

  _____

- Ask her politely how much it costs.

  _____

Discovering
FRENCH *Nouveau!*

B L E U

LEÇON 4 De jour en jour Vidéo-scène A. L'heure

LISTENING ACTIVITIES

Section 1. Quelle heure est-il? (Part 1)

A. Compréhension orale

▶

1. 2. 3. 4. 5.

B. Questions et réponses

▶

1. Il est dix
heures.   2. . . . midi.   3. . . . une heure.   4. . . . trois heures.

▶

Quelle heure est-il?

Il est
huit heures.

5. . . . quatre
heures.   6. . . . neuf
heures.   7. . . . minuit.

Section 2. Quelle heure est-il? (Part 2)

C. Compréhension orale

▶

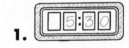
1.

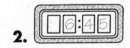
2.

3.

4.

Nom _____

Classe _____ Date _____

Discovering
FRENCH
Nouveau!

B L E U

D. Questions et réponses

 1. Il est dix heures et quart.

 2. . . . onze heures et demie.

 3. . . . deux heures moins le quart.

 4. . . . six heures dix.

 5. . . . neuf heures vingt.

 6. . . . dix heures quarante.

Section 3. À quelle heure?

E. Compréhension orale

▶   le film   4 h 15

1. la classe de français   11h

2. le dîner   7h30

3. le film   9h10

4. le train de Toulouse   5h45

Section 4. Dictée

F. Écoutez et écrivez.

—Dis, Philippe, quelle _heure_ est-il?

—Il _est_ cinq heures _moins_ le quart.

—Et à quelle heure est le film?

—À sept heures et _demie_.

—Merci!

Nom _____

Classe _____ Date _____

Discovering
FRENCH
Nouveau!
BLEU

Unité 2
Leçon 4
Workbook TE

WRITING ACTIVITIES

1. Oui ou non?

Watches do not always work well. Read the times below and compare them with the times indicated on the watches. If the two times match, check **oui**. If they do not match, check **non**.

	oui	non
▶ Il est une heure dix.	☑	☐
▶ Il est une heure vingt-cinq.	☐	☑
1. Il est deux heures et demie.	☑	☐
2. Il est trois heures et quart.	☑	☐
3. Il est cinq heures moins vingt.	☐	☑
4. Il est sept heures moins le quart.	☑	☐
5. Il est huit heures cinq.	☑	☐
6. Il est onze heures cinquante-cinq.	☐	☑

Super Écran
VENDREDI 22 MARS

14h50	Lawrence d'Arabie
18h20	Oncle Buck
20h05	Les Simpson
21h00	Tremors
22h40	Miss Daisy et Son Chauffeur

FLASH culturel

In many French-speaking countries, official time is given using a 24-hour clock. For example, on this Canadian TV schedule, the movie *Driving Miss Daisy* begins at 22 h 40 (**vingt-deux heures quarante**). What would be the corresponding time on our 12-hour clock?

☐ 2:40 P.M.   ☐ 8:40 P.M.   ☐ 9:40 P.M.   ☑ 10:40 P.M.

→page 44

Nom _____

Classe _____ Date _____

Discovering
FRENCH
Nouveau!

B L E U

2. Quelle heure est-il?

Stéphanie's watch is not working. Tell her what time it is. Write out your responses.

 1. Il est une heure _____

_____.

 4. *Il est sept heures et demie*

(sept heures trente) .

 2. Il est midi _____

_____.

 5. *Il est neuf heures moins le quart*

(huit heures quarante-cinq) .

3:15 3. Il est trois heures et quart

(trois heures quinze) .

 6. *Il est dix heures cinquante*

(onze heures moins dix) .

3. Communication: En français! *(sample answers)*

A. *Conversation avec Caroline*   You are in a café with your friend Caroline. You plan to see a movie together. Complete the dialogue.

CAROLINE: Quelle heure est-il?

YOU: *Il est [deux heures et quart].* _____
(Look at your watch and tell her the time.)

CAROLINE: À quelle heure est le film?

YOU: *À [trois heures moins le quart].* _____
(Name a time about half an hour from now.)

B. *Conversation avec Julien*   You are in a hurry to keep an appointment with Mme Pascal, your math teacher. You meet your friend Julien. Complete the dialogue.

YOU: *Quelle heure est-il?* _____
(Ask Julien what time it is.)

JULIEN: Il est onze heures dix. Pourquoi *(why)*?

YOU: *J'ai un rendez-vous* avec Madame Pascal.
(Say you have an appointment with Madame Pascal.)

JULIEN: À quelle heure?

YOU: *À onze heures et quart. Au revoir, Julien.* _____
(Tell him at quarter past eleven, and say good-bye.)

FLASH culturel

With the 24-hour clock, times are expressed as follows:

- A.M. hours go from 0 h 01 (one minute after midnight) to 12 h 00 (noon).
- P.M. hours go from 12 h 01 to 24 h 00.

To calculate the P.M. equivalent of 24-hour clock times, simply subtract 12.

22 h 40 =
22:40−12 =
10:40 P.M.

Discovering
FRENCH
Nouveau!

BLEU

Unité 2
Leçon 4

Workbook TE

Vidéo-scène B. Le jour et la date

LISTENING ACTIVITIES

Section 1. Les jours de la semaine

A. Compréhension orale Listening comprehension

▶ Christine arrive mardi.

▶ Christine

1. Pauline
2. Bertrand
3. Céline
4. Didier
5. Agnès
6. Guillaume
7. Véronique

a. lundi
b. mardi
c. mercredi
d. jeudi
e. vendredi
f. samedi
g. dimanche

Section 2. La date

B. Compréhension orale

▶ C'est le _2_ février.

1. C'est le _22_ mars.
2. C'est le _3_ juin.
3. C'est le _1_ juillet.
4. C'est le _8_ août.
5. C'est le _3_ septembre.
6. C'est le _4_ novembre.

Nom _____

Classe _____ Date _____

C. Questions et réponses

 —Quel jour est-ce?
—C'est le 5 décembre.

  1.  2.  3.

 4.  5.  6.  7.

Section 3. L'anniversaire

D. Compréhension orale

▶ Alice:	le _18/7_
1. Béatrice:	le _23/12_
2. Françoise:	le _1/3_
3. Julie:	le _13/5_
4. Delphine:	le _29/6_
5. Denis:	le _6/11_
6. Paul:	le _15/8_

Nom _____

Classe _____ Date _____

Discovering
FRENCH
Nouveau!

BLEU

Unité 2
Leçon 4

Workbook TE

Section 4. Conversations

E. Compréhension orale

1. What day is it today?
   a. Tuesday
   b. Wednesday
   c. Friday

2. When is Charlotte's birthday?
   a. in March
   b. in October
   c. in December

3. When is David's birthday?
   a. in January
   b. in August
   c. in September

4. When will David and Charlotte meet again?
   a. tomorrow
   b. tonight
   c. in a week

Section 5. Dictée

F. Écoutez et écrivez.

—C'est quand, ton _anniversaire_ ?

—C'est le deux _juin_ . C'est un _dimanche_ . Et toi?

—Moi, c'est le _premier_ novembre. C'est un _vendredi_ .

Nom _____

Classe _____ Date _____

WRITING ACTIVITIES

1. La semaine

Can you fit the seven days of the week into the following French puzzle?

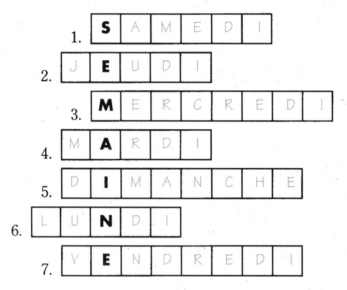

1. **S** A M E D I
2. J **E** U D I
3. **M** E R C R E D I
4. M **A** R D I
5. D **I** M A N C H E
6. L U **N** D I
7. V **E** N D R E D I

2. Les mois

Complete the grid with the names of the missing months.

janvier	février	mars
avril	mai	juin
juillet	août	septembre
octobre	novembre	décembre

FLASH culturel

In France, **le quatorze juillet** is a very important date. What do the French do on that day?

❏ They vote.   ☑ They celebrate their national holiday.

❏ They pay their taxes.   ❏ They honor their war veterans.

➡**page 49**

Nom _____

Classe _____ Date _____

Discovering
FRENCH
Nouveau!

BLEU

Unité 2
Leçon 4

Workbook TE

3. Joyeux anniversaire! *(Happy birthday!)* (sample answers)

Ask five friends when their birthdays are. Write out the information in French on the chart below.

NOM	ANNIVERSAIRE
▶ David	le trois juillet
1. Gail	le douze mai
2. Randy	le vingt-cinq septembre
3. Ines	le treize décembre
4. Alex	le premier octobre
5. Charlene	le trente avril

4. 👥 Communication: En français! (sample answers)

Answer the following questions in complete sentences.

1. Quel jour est-ce aujourd'hui?

   Aujourd'hui, c'est [jeudi].

2. Et demain?

   Demain, c'est [vendredi].

3. Quelle est la date aujourd'hui?

   C'est le [7 mai].

4. C'est quand, ton anniversaire?

   Mon anniversaire est le [18 février].

Fête Nationale
mardi 14 juillet
à 22h
PARIS

FLASH culturel

On July 14, or "Bastille Day" as it is known in the United States, the French celebrate their national holiday. On July 14, 1789, a Parisian mob stormed **la Bastille**, a state prison which had come to symbolize the king's tyranny. This important historical event marked the beginning of the French Revolution and led to the establishment of a republican form of government for the first time in French history.

Nom _____

Classe _____ Date _____

Discovering
FRENCH
Nouveau!

B L E U

Unité 2
Leçon 4

Workbook TE

Vidéo-scène C. Le temps

LISTENING ACTIVITIES

Section 1. Quel temps fait-il?

A. Compréhension orale

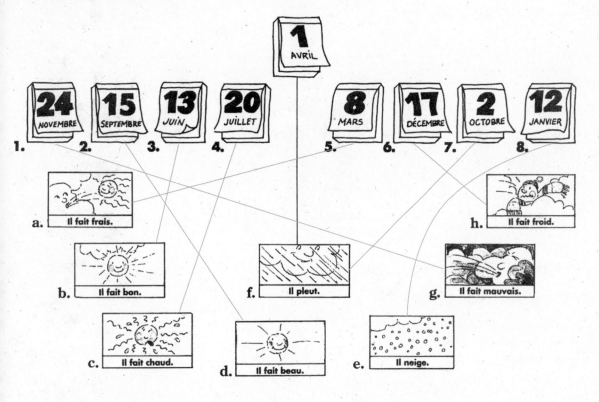

1. 24 NOVEMBRE
2. 15 SEPTEMBRE
3. 13 JUIN
4. 20 JUILLET

1 AVRIL

5. 8 MARS
6. 17 DÉCEMBRE
7. 2 OCTOBRE
8. 12 JANVIER

a. Il fait frais.
b. Il fait bon.
c. Il fait chaud.
d. Il fait beau.
e. Il neige.
f. Il pleut.
g. Il fait mauvais.
h. Il fait froid.

BLEU

B. Questions et réponses

Il fait chaud..   Il fait froid.   Il fait beau.

Il fait mauvais.   Il pleut.   Il neige.

Section 2. Conversations

C. Compréhension orale

1. What does Jean-Paul want to know?
   a. what the weather is like
   b. what day it is
   c. what time it is

2. How is the weather today?
   a. It is nice.
   b. It is cold.
   c. It is warm.

3. How is the weather in Paris?
   a. It is raining.
   b. It is snowing.
   c. It is hot.

4. What is Jean-Paul's favorite season?
   a. spring
   b. summer
   c. fall

Section 3. Dictée

D. Écoutez et écrivez.

—Quel _temps_ fait-il aujourd'hui?

—Il fait _beau_ .

—Et en _automne_ ?

—Il _pleut_ .

WRITING ACTIVITIES

1. Les quatre saisons

Write the names of the seasons associated with the following pictures.

l'été _____ l'hiver _____ l'automne _____ le printemps _____

2. La météo *(Weather report)*

Look at the map of France and describe the weather in the cities indicated below.

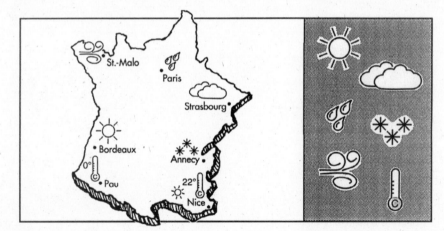

1. À Pau, _il fait froid_____.

2. À Nice, _il fait beau (chaud, bon)_____.

3. À Bordeaux, _il fait beau (bon)_____.

4. À Strasbourg, _il fait mauvais_____.

5. À Annecy, _il neige_____.

6. À St-Malo, _il fait frais_____.

7. À Paris, _il pleut_____.

---

*F*LASH culturel

If you went to France for Christmas vacation, what kind of weather should you expect?

☑ rain   ☑ snow   ☑ cold weather   ☑ mild weather

➜ **page 54**

URB
p. 77

Discovering
FRENCH
Nouveau!

B L E U

3. Communication: Quel temps fait-il? (sample answers)

Describe the weather in the city where you live.

1. Aujourd'hui, *il fait beau* .
2. En été, *il fait chaud* .
3. En automne, *il fait frais* .
4. En hiver, *il fait mauvais* .
5. Au printemps, *il pleut* .

4. Communication: As-tu faim? As-tu soif? (sample answers)

When we go to a café, what we order often depends on the weather. Read each of the
weather descriptions and then indicate what you would like to eat and/or drink.

Le Temps	Au Café
	S'il vous plaît, . . .
▶ Il fait froid.	donnez-moi *un croissant et un chocolat*
1. Il fait chaud.	donnez-moi *une glace à la vanille et un soda* .
2. Il pleut.	donnez-moi *un hot dog et un jus de raisin* .
3. Il neige.	donnez-moi *une omelette et un thé* .
4. Il fait frais.	donnez-moi *une pizza et une limonade* .

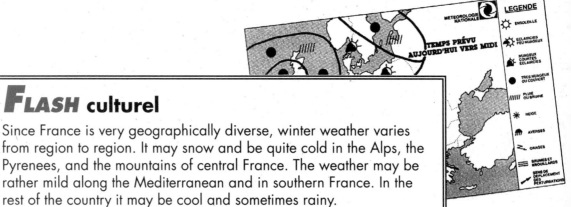

*F*LASH culturel

Since France is very geographically diverse, winter weather varies
from region to region. It may snow and be quite cold in the Alps, the
Pyrenees, and the mountains of central France. The weather may be
rather mild along the Mediterranean and in southern France. In the
rest of the country it may be cool and sometimes rainy.

Discovering
FRENCH *Nouveau!*

BLEU

Unité 2
Leçon 4A

Activités pour tous TE

LEÇON 4A   L'heure

A

Activité 1   Dialogue

Select the words that best complete the dialogue.

—Salut, Brigitte. On va dans un café?
—Oui, *merci /(d'accord.)* Mais quelle heure *c'est /(est-il?)*
—*(Il est)/ C'est* deux heures et demie.
—Bon.*(J'ai)/ Je suis* une heure.

Activité 2   Quand?

When are the following activities taking place?

	a. le matin	b. l'après-midi	c. le soir

c   1. Le concert de rock est à huit heures et demie.

a   2. Le rendez-vous chez le dentiste est à dix heures et quart.

a   3. L'examen de maths est à neuf heures.

b   4. Le rendez-vous au café est à une heure.

Activité 3 L'heure

Your friend George is always ten minutes late. If he is due to arrive at the times shown on the watch, when will he probably arrive? Circle the correct answers.

1.

   une heure /
   une heure dix

2.

   deux heures et quart /
   une heure moins cinq

3. [watch: 4:35]

   quatre heures et demie /
   cinq heures moins le quart

B

Activité 1 Questions et réponses

Match the answers to the questions.

c   1. Quelle heure est-il?   a. Il est à 8h.

a   2. À quelle heure est le film?   b. Non, il est à 2h.

b   3. Le match est à une heure?   c. Il est 10h.

Nom _____

Classe _____ Date _____ _____

Discovering
FRENCH
Nouveau!
B L E U

Activité 2 Dialogues

Circle the correct expressions.

1. Le film est à huit heures *du soir* / *de l'après-midi*.

2. Le train pour New York est à sept heures *de l'après-midi* / *du matin*.

3. Le match de hockey est à deux heures *du matin* / *de l'après-midi*.

Activité 3 Les cours

What time do Stéphanie's classes start? Write down the times.

français   *histoire*   *géométrie*

à _huit heures vingt-cinq_   à _neuf heures et demie_   à _onze heures moins le quart_

C

Activité 1 Questions

Mélanie and Sophie are talking about Sophie's plans for the day. Write the questions that would produce the following responses.

1. — _Quelle heure est-il?_____

   —Il est dix heures du matin.

2. — _À quelle heure est ton rendez vous?_____

   —Mon rendez-vous est à deux heures.

3. — _À quelle heure est le film?_____

   —Le film est à huit heures.

Activité 2 L'heure

State whether the following times are in the morning, afternoon, or evening.

1.   2.   3.

Il est dix heures   Il est trois heures   Ma famille dîne à sept heures
du matin   .   _de l'après midi_   .   _du soir_   .

Activité 3 Ma journée (sample answers)

Write out the times you typically do the following activities.

1. get up _à sept heures_____

2. eat breakfast _à sept heures dix_____

3. go to school _à sept heures et demie_____

Nom _____

Classe _____ Date _____

Discovering
FRENCH
Nouveau!

BLEU

Unité 2
Leçon 4B

Activités pour tous TE

LEÇON 4B Le jour et la date

A

Activité 1 Dialogue

Select the words that best complete the dialogues.

—Quelle est (la date) / le jour, aujourd'hui?

—(Aujourd'hui,) / Demain, c'est le un / (le premier) avril.

—C'est ton anniversaire?

—Non, (mon) / ton anniversaire est aujourd'hui / (demain.)

Activité 2 Les mois

Tell what month the following events take place.

Modèle: (Super Bowl)	C'est en janvier.
(Halloween)	C'est en octobre.
(Mother's Day)	C'est en mai.
(Bastille Day)	C'est en juillet.
(Christmas)	C'est en décembre.

Activité 3 La date

Circle the date in French that does not fit in with the others because it is out of season.

1. 10/01   (03/05)   05/02   3. 01/10   06/09   (02/01)

2. 02/04   07/05   (08/10)   4. (05/02)   04/08   12/07

B

Activité 1 Questions et réponses

Select the best answer to each question.

_c_ 1. —Quelle est la date, aujourd'hui?   a. —C'est demain.

_a_ 2. —C'est quand, ton anniversaire?   b. —C'est mercredi.

_b_ 3. —Quel jour est-ce aujourd'hui?   c. —C'est le deux novembre.

Activité 2 L'intrus

Which words do not belong with the others?

1. jeudi / dimanche / (août)   4. demain / aujourd'hui / (mai)
2. (le vingt) / janvier / juillet   5. le premier / (mars) / le treize
3. vendredi / (le seize) / jeudi

Discovering
FRENCH
Nouveau!

B L E U

Nom _____

Classe _____ Date _____

Activité 3 La date

Match the date associated with the following people or events.

<u>c</u> 1. le trente et un octobre   a. George Washington's Birthday

<u>d</u> 2. le premier avril   b. Bastille Day

<u>a</u> 3. le vingt-deux février   c. Halloween

<u>b</u> 4. le quatorze juillet   d. April Fool's Day (Poisson d'avril)

C

Activité 1 Quel jour est-ce?

Your friend is off by a day. Answer the questions.

1. —Aujourd'hui, c'est mardi? —Non, *c'est mercredi.*

2. —L'examen de science, c'est aujourd'hui? —Non, *c'est demain.*

3. —Ton anniversaire, c'est le vingt? —Non, *c'est le vingt et un.*

Activité 2 La poste

Write out the dates that these letters were mailed.

1.

le douze février deux mille un

3.

le premier mai deux mille un

2.

le dix août deux mille

4.

le cinq janvier deux mille deux

Activité 3 La date

Write the day and date that is two days later than the one given.

1. le vendredi douze juin   *le dimanche quatorze juin*

2. le mardi trente et un octobre   *le jeudi deux novembre*

3. le jeudi dix-neuf août   *le samedi vingt et un août*

Nom _____

Classe _____ Date _____

Discovering
FRENCH
Nouveau!
BLEU

Unité 2
Leçon 4C

Activités pour tous TE

LEÇON 4C Le temps

A

Activité 1 Le temps

Circle the words that complete the dialogue.

—Quel temps (fait-il) / est-ce?

—(Il pleut.) / Il est trois heures.

—(Pas possible!) / À quelle heure?

—(Pourquoi?) / L'après-midi.

—Parce que le match de (tennis) / hockey est (aujourd'hui) / demain!

Activité 2 Les saisons

Match the seasons with the following dates in French.

le printemps	l'été	l'automne	l'hiver

1. le quatre juillet   l'été

2. le vingt-cinq décembre   l'hiver

3. le vingt-huit novembre   l'automne

4. le quinze juin   le printemps

Activité 3 La météo

Circle the most logical weather expression for each activity.

1.
2.
3.
4.

1. Il fait frais.
   (Il fait chaud.)

2. (Il fait froid.)
   Il pleut.

3. Il fait mauvais.
   (Il neige.)

4. (Il fait bon.)
   Il fait froid.

B

Activité 1 Questions et réponses

Choose the best answer to each question.

1. —Quel temps fait-il aujourd'hui?
   —(Il fait beau.) / C'est l'hiver.

   —Et demain?
   —(Il fait bon aussi.) / C'est le printemps.

2. —En quelle saison est le Super Bowl?
   —(En hiver.) / Au printemps.

3. —On va au café aujourd'hui?
   —(Non, il pleut!) / Oui, il neige.

Nom _____

Classe _____ Date _____

Activité 2 La météo

Circle the *best* word or expression for each picture.

1.

Il fait beau.
Il fait mauvais.
(Il pleut.)

2.

Il fait chaud.
(Il fait froid.)
Il fait frais.

3.

(Il neige.)
Il fait froid.
Il pleut.

4.

Il fait chaud.
Il fait mauvais.
(Il fait beau.)

Activité 3 Questions

Determine whether the following terms refer to the weather, seasons, or days.

c	1. dimanche	
a	2. il pleut	
a	3. il fait beau	

b	4. le printemps
c	5. mercredi
b	6. l'été

a. la météo
b. les saisons
c. les jours

C

Activité 1 Le temps

Write two sentences that describe the weather conditions in the areas given.

1. Quel temps fait-il à Québec en hiver? _Il fait froid._

2. Quel temps fait-il à Orlando en été? _Il fait chaud._

3. Quel temps fait-il à Seattle au printemps? _Il pleut._

Activité 2 Catégories

Write the words from the following list under the appropriate heading.

Il fait mauvais.   dimanche   Il neige.   janvier
l'été   vendredi   août   le printemps

la météo	les saisons	les jours	les mois
Il fait mauvais.	l'été	dimanche	janvier
Il neige.	le printemps	vendredi	août

Activité 3 La météo

For each picture, write two short sentences stating the season and weather condition.

1.

C'est l'automne.
Il pleut.

2.

C'est l'été.
Il fait chaud.

3.

C'est hiver.
Il neige.

4.

C'est le printemps.
Il fait frais.

LEÇON 4A   L'heure, page 56

Objectives

Communicative Functions and Topics
To ask for and indicate the time, including hours, half hours, quarter hours, and minutes
To ask and say when certain events are scheduled
To talk about appointments or dates

Linguistic Goals
To use question expressions for time: *Quelle heure* and *À quelle heure*
To respond to questions about time: *Il est, À*

Cultural Goals
To learn about the French 24-hour clock system

Motivation and Focus

❑ Have students look at the photos on page 56 and suggest where the characters are and what time it is. Ask them to identify typical daily and weekend activities and corresponding times for the activities.

❑ Play section 4a.5 of the **Video**, or read that section in the **Videoscript**, page 9. Discuss *L'heure officielle*. Explain the CROSS-CULTURAL OBSERVATION, page 57 of the TE. Ask students to think about places in the U.S. where the 24-hour time system is used.

Presentation and Explanation

❑ *Lesson Opener:* Use the WARM-UP activity on page 56 of the TE to review numbers. To present the opening conversation, model or play **Audio** CD 1, Tracks 37–38. Replay with students reading along. Then discuss what they think the conversation is about.

❑ *Pour communiquer:* Introduce asking the time and telling time with **Overhead Transparency** 6. Discuss the information in the boxes on pages 56–58. Use **Audio** CD 1, Tracks 40–41 or model conversation 2 on page 58. Then read and discuss it with the students. Present the information in the box on page 58.

Guided Practice and Checking Understanding

❑ Practice telling time using the Description on page A53 and the Goal 2 activity on page A54 of **Overhead Transparencies**, and with the COMPREHENSION Activities on pages 57 and 58 of the TE.

❑ Use the **Audioscript** or the **Audio** CD 6, Tracks 16–21 to do Listening Activities A–F in the **Workbook** on pages 41–42.

❑ Play the **Video** or read the **Videoscript** as students do **Video Activities** 1–6, pages 103–105. Go over the answers with the class.

Independent Practice

❑ Model Activities 1–5 on pages 57 and 59 before having students work in pairs to practice them. Play **Audio** CD 1, Track 39 with Activity 1. Use **Overhead Transparency** 1 to do the GEOGRAPHY SKILLS Activity, page 59 of the TE, before practicing asking and answering questions about train schedules in Activity 6, page 59.

❑ Students can work on **Teacher to Teacher** page 4 to practice time expressions.

❑ Use any or all of *Conversations 3–4, Échange 2,* or *Tête à tête 2* in **Communipak**, pages 138, 140, 143, and 148–149. Arrange students in pairs or groups to practice and present their conversations to the class. Students can also work in pairs to practice talking about train schedules using **Video Activities** page 106.

❑ Have students do any appropriate activities in **Activités pour tous,** pages 23–24.

URB
p. 85

Monitoring and Adjusting

❏ As students work on the activities on pages 57 and 59, monitor their use of time expressions. Refer them to the expressions and explanations in *Pour communiquer* on pages 56–58 as needed.

❏ Have students do **Workbook** Writing Activities on pages 43–44.

Reteaching

❏ Redo activities in the **Workbook** that correspond to language items that students may be finding difficult.

❏ Students can use the **Video** to review portions of the lesson.

Summary and Closure

❏ Help students use the two dialogues in this lesson as models to create their own dialogues about time and appointments. Students can present the dialogues to the class, or they can be videotaped for inclusion in students' Oral Portfolios.

Unité 2
Leçon 4

Lesson Plans

Discovering
FRENCH
Nouveau!

BLEU

LEÇON 4B Le jour et la date, page 60

Objectives

Communicative Functions and Topics
To talk about days of the week
To tell people when you will see them again
To talk about the date
To talk about birthdays

Linguistic Goals
To express a date in French
To use casual question forms: *C'est quand?*

Cultural Goals
To compare date patterns in French and English

Motivation and Focus

❑ Have students share birthdays to prepare them for the focus on the lesson.
❑ Play **Video** 4b.3, *Joyeux anniversaire!*, or read the **Videoscript**. Discuss students' impressions of French birthday celebrations.

Presentation and Explanation

❑ *Lesson Opener:* Use the WARM-UP AND REVIEW activity on page 60 of the TE to provide practice with expressing feelings. Model or present dialogues 1 and 2 with **Video** or **Audio** CD 1, Tracks 42–45. Pause to encourage student comments on the conversations and situations. Have students read the conversations and discuss what is being said.
❑ *Pour communiquer:* Introduce and practice days of the week and the expressions in the box on page 61 with **Overhead Transparency** 9. Explain the CULTURAL NOTE in the margin of page 61 of the TE. Present months of the year and expressions for talking about dates in *Pour communiquer* on page 62 with the same transparency. Explain the pattern used in French to express dates, as presented in the grammar box on page 63.

Guided Practice and Checking Understanding

❑ Practice talking about days and dates with **Overhead Transparency** 9. Discuss the French calendar with the Goal 2 Activity on page A59.
❑ To check understanding, use the **Audioscript** or **Audio** CD 6, Tracks 22–27 and **Workbook** Listening Activities A–F, pages 45–47.
❑ Play the **Video**, or read the **Videoscript**, as students do pages 107–109 in the **Video Activities**.

Independent Practice

❑ Model and have students repeat the practice Activities on pages 61 and 63. Activities 1, 2, 3, and 6 can be done for homework and 4 and 5 in pairs.
❑ Arrange students in pairs to practice asking and answering questions about birthdays and dates with **Communipak** *Interviews* 1–4, *Conversation* 1, *Échange* 1, or *Tête à tête* 3 (pages 132–151), or **Video Activities** *Activité* 6, page 110.
❑ Have students do any appropriate activities in **Activités pour tous**, pages 25–26.

Monitoring and Adjusting

❑ Have students work on Writing Activities 1–4 on pages 48–49 in the **Workbook**.
❑ Monitor students' understanding as they work on the practice activities. Have them study the expressions and vocabulary in the *Pour communiquer* boxes on pages 61–62 and the grammar box on page 63.

URB
p. 87

BLEU

Reteaching

❑ Have students redo any of the **Workbook** activities with which they had difficulty.
❑ Reteach birthdays, days, and dates using either of the following: Variation Activity 4, page 63 of the TE, or **Teacher to Teacher**, page 5.
❑ Assign the **Video** for students who need review.

Discovering
FRENCH
Nouveau!

BLEU

Unité 2
Leçon 4
Lesson Plans

LEÇON 4C Le temps, page 64

Objectives

Communicative Functions and Topics
To talk about the weather
To use weather expressions
To identify seasons

Linguistic Goals To use *il fait* to talk about weather

Cultural Goals To learn about climates in various regions of France

Motivation and Focus

❏ Have students look at the map of France on page 4 and do the GEOGRAPHY ACTIVITY and PRE-VIEWING ACTIVITY, page 65 of the TE. Play the **Video** or read the **Videoscript** for section 4C.3 to introduce the climate of the different provinces, using the map on **Overhead Transparency** 1.

Presentation and Explanation

❏ *Lesson Opener:* Use the WARM-UP AND REVIEW Activity on page 64 of the TE to practice months and dates. With books closed, act out or use **Video** or **Audio** CD 1, Tracks 46–47 to present the opening conversation. Ask students to read and summarize the conversation.

❏ *Pour communiquer:* Introduce and practice describing weather conditions with **Overhead Transparency** 13. Point out and have students repeat the expressions and names of the seasons in the *Pour communiquer* box, page 65.

Guided Practice and Checking Understanding

❏ Use **Overhead Transparency** 13 and the Activity on page A63 to practice weather expressions.

❏ To check understanding, use the **Audio** CD 6, Tracks 28–31 or read the **Audioscript** as students do **Workbook** Listening Activities A–D, pages 51–52.

❏ Play the **Video** or read the **Videoscript** and have students do **Video Activities** pages 111–113.

❏ Practice weather expressions using the COMPREHENSION Activity on page 65 of the TE.

Independent Practice

❏ Have students do Activities 1 and 2 on page 65 individually and check their answers.

❏ Use any of the following activities for pair practice in talking about the weather: **Communipak** *Interview* 2, *Tu as la parole* 3 and 4, *Conversation* 3, *Échange* 2, or *Tête à tête* 2 (pages 133–149); or **Video Activities** page 114.

❏ Have students do any appropriate activities in **Activités pour tous,** pages 27–28.

Monitoring and Adjusting

❏ Assign **Workbook** Writing Activities 1–4, pages 53–54.

❏ Monitor students' use of weather expressions as they do the practice activities. Remind them to look at the *Pour communiquer* box on page 65 of the text as needed.

Unité 2
Leçon 4

Lesson Plans

Discovering
FRENCH
Nouveau!

BLEU

End-of-Lesson Activities

❑ *À votre tour!:* Choose any or all of the Activities on pages 66–67. Students can use the **Audio** CD 1, Tracks 48–49 to check their responses for Activities 1 and 3. Arrange students in pairs/groups to practice and present the role plays in Activities 4–5. Activity 6 can be done as a whole-class activity. Use the CHALLENGE ACTIVITY on page 67 of the TE to practice using language from this and previous units.

Reteaching

❑ Have students redo any appropriate activities in the **Workbook**.
❑ Reteach weather expressions using **Teacher to Teacher** page 6.
❑ Assign the **Video** for students who need to do review or makeup work.

Assessment

❑ Use Quiz 4 on pages 129–130 after students have completed the lesson. Unit Test 2 (Form A or B) on pages 165–170 can be used as a comprehensive assessment of the unit's goals and objectives. Choose any or all of the **Performance Tests** as needed for additional assessment of specific language skills. The **Test Generator** can be used to modify test questions to meet your particular needs.

Summary and Closure

❑ Show **Overhead Transparency** 1 and ask students to point out and talk about the climate of the regions of France that were studied in the lesson. Summarize information about the climate of French geographical regions and weather conditions.

End-of-Unit Activities

Note: These activities may be done at the end of the unit, or at any appropriate time during the unit.

❑ *Entracte 2:* Introduce parts of the body with the COMPREHENSION Activity on page 68 of the TE. Read *Un jeu: Jacques a dit* on page 68 and play the game. You may also wish to play the GAME described in the margin on page 68 of the TE. Introduce the song *Alouette* with the PRE-READING ACTIVITY on page 69 of the TE. Share the cultural note with the class, sing the song, and do the POST-READING ACTIVITY.
❑ *Reading and Culture Activities:* Assign **Workbook** activities A–C, pages 55–57. Go over the answers with the class.

Discovering
FRENCH
Nouveau!

BLEU

Unité 2
Leçon 4

Block Scheduling
Lesson Plans

LEÇON 4A   L'heure, page 56

Block Scheduling (2 Days to Complete)

Objectives

Communicative Functions and Topics   To ask for and indicate the time, including hours, half hours, quarter hours, and minutes
To ask and say when certain events are scheduled
To talk about appointments or dates

Linguistic Goals   To use question expressions for time: *Quelle heure* and *À quelle heure*
To respond to questions about time: *Il est, À*

Cultural Goals   To learn about the French 24-hour clock system

Block Schedule

Change of Pace Bring in copies of the movie listings from your local newspaper. Tell students the name of the movie theater and say in French the time a movie begins. Have students race to be the first to identify the movie. ■

Day 1

Motivation and Focus

❏ Have students look at the photos on page 56 and suggest where the characters are and what time it is. Ask them to identify typical daily and weekend activities and corresponding times for the activities.

❏ Play section 4a.5 of the **Video**, or read that section in the **Videoscript**, page 9. Discuss *L'heure officielle*. Explain the Cross-cultural observation, page 57 of the TE. Ask students to think about places in the U.S. where the 24-hour time system is used.

Presentation and Explanation

❏ *Lesson Opener:* Use the Warm-up activity on page 56 of the TE to review numbers. To present the opening conversation, model or play **Audio** CD 1, Tracks 37–38. Replay with students reading along. Then discuss what they think the conversation is about.

❏ *Pour communiquer:* Introduce asking the time and telling time with **Overhead Transparency** 6. Discuss the information in the boxes on pages 56–58. Use **Audio** CD 1, Tracks 40–41 or model conversation 2 on page 58. Then read and discuss it with the students. Present the information in the box on page 58.

Guided Practice and Checking Understanding

❏ Practice telling time using the Description on page A53 and the Goal 2 activity on page A54 of **Overhead Transparencies**, and with the Comprehension Activities on pages 57 and 58 of the TE.

❏ Have students do the **Block Schedule Activity** at the top of this page.

❏ Use **Block Scheduling Copymasters** 25–32.

❏ Use the **Audioscript** or **Audio** CD 6, Tracks 16–21 to do Listening Activities A–F in the **Workbook** on pages 41–42.

❏ Play the **Video** or read the **Videoscript** as students do **Video Activities** 1–6, pages 103–105. Go over the answers with the class.

Unité 2
Leçon 4

Block Scheduling
Lesson Plans

Discovering
FRENCH
Nouveau!

B L E U

Independent Practice

❑ Model Activities 1–5 on pages 57 and 59 before having students work in pairs to practice them. Play **Audio** CD 1, Track 39 with Activity 1. Use **Overhead Transparency** 1 to do the Geography skills Activity, page 59 of the TE, before practicing asking and answering questions about train schedules in Activity 6, page 59.

❑ Students can work on **Teacher to Teacher** page 4 to practice time expressions.

❑ Use any or all of *Conversations* 3–4, *Échange* 2, or *Tête à tête* 2 in **Communipak**, pages 138, 140, 143, and 148–149. Arrange students in pairs or groups to practice and present their conversations to the class. Students can also work in pairs to practice talking about train schedules using **Video Activities** page 106.

❑ Have students do any appropriate activities in **Activités pour tous**, pages 25–26.

Day 2

Monitoring and Adjusting

❑ As students work on the activities on pages 57 and 59, monitor their use of time expressions. Refer them to the expressions and explanations in *Pour communiquer* on pages 56–58 as needed.

❑ Have students do **Workbook** Writing Activities on pages 43–44.

Reteaching (as needed)

❑ Redo activities in the **Workbook** that correspond to language items that students may be finding difficult.

❑ Students can use the **Video** to review portions of the lesson.

Summary and Closure

❑ Help students use the two dialogues in this vidéo-scène as models to create their own dialogues about time and appointments. Students can present the dialogues to the class, or they can be videotaped for inclusion in students' Oral Portfolios.

Discovering
FRENCH
Nouveau!

BLEU

Unité 2
Leçon 4
Block Scheduling
Lesson Plans

LEÇON 4B Le jour et la date, page 60

Block Scheduling (2 Days to Complete)

Objectives

Communicative Functions and Topics	To talk about days of the week
	To tell people when you will see them again
	To talk about the date
	To talk about birthdays
Linguistic Goals	To express a date in French
	To use casual question forms: *C'est quand?*
Cultural Goals	To compare date patterns in French and English

Block Schedule

Fun Break Give a time limit of five minutes. Have students arrange themselves in order from the youngest student to the oldest by asking and telling the date on which they were born. ■

Day 1

Motivation and Focus

❑ Have students share birthdays to prepare them for the focus on the lesson.
❑ Play **Video** 4b.3, *Joyeux anniversaire!*, or read the **Videoscript**. Discuss students' impressions of French birthday celebrations.

Presentation and Explanation

❑ *Lesson Opener:* Use the WARM-UP AND REVIEW activity on page 60 of the TE to provide practice with expressing feelings. Model or present dialogues 1 and 2 with **Video** or **Audio** CD 1, Tracks 42–45. Pause to encourage student comments on the conversations and situations. Have students read the conversations and discuss what is being said.
❑ *Pour communiquer:* Introduce and practice days of the week and the expressions in the box on page 61 with **Overhead Transparency** 9. Explain the CULTURAL NOTE in the margin of page 61 of the TE. Present months of the year and expressions for talking about dates in *Pour communiquer* on page 62 with the same transparency. Explain the pattern used in French to express dates, as presented in the grammar box on page 63.

Guided Practice and Checking Understanding

❑ Practice talking about days and dates with **Overhead Transparency** 9. Discuss the French calendar with the Goal 2 activity on page A59.
❑ Have students do the **Block Schedule Activity** at the top of this page.
❑ Use **Block Scheduling Copymasters** 25–32.
❑ To check understanding, use the **Audioscript** or **Audio** CD 6, Tracks 22–27 and **Workbook** Listening Activities A–F, pages 45–47.
❑ Play the **Video** or read the **Videoscript** as students do pages 107–109 in the **Video Activities**.

Day 2

Independent Practice

❑ Model and have students repeat the practice activities on pages 61 and 63. Activities 1, 2, 3, and 6 can be done for homework and 4 and 5 in pairs.

❑ Arrange students in pairs to practice asking and answering questions about birthdays and dates with **Communipak** *Interviews* 1–4, *Conversation* 1, *Échange* 1, or *Tête à tête* 3 (pages 132–151), or **Video Activities** Activité 6, page 110.

❑ Have students do any appropriate activities in **Activités pour tous,** pages 25–26.

Monitoring and Adjusting

❑ Have students work on Writing Activities 1–4 on pages 48–49 in the **Workbook**.

❑ Monitor students' understanding as they work on the practice activities. Have them study the expressions and vocabulary in the *Pour communiquer* boxes on pages 61–62 and the grammar box on page 63.

Reteaching (as needed)

❑ Have students redo any of the **Workbook** activities with which they had difficulty.

❑ Reteach birthdays, days, and dates using either of the following: VARIATION Activity 4, page 63 of the TE, or **Teacher to Teacher**, page 5.

❑ Assign the **Video** for students who need review.

Summary and Closure

❑ Give groups of students a calendar with which to look up the day of the week their birthday falls on this year. Have students take turns asking and telling the day their birthday will be on.

Discovering
FRENCH
Nouveau!

BLEU

Unité 2
Leçon 4

Block Scheduling
Lesson Plans

LEÇON 4C Le temps, page 64

Block Scheduling (3 Days to Complete—including Unit Test)

Objectives

Communicative Functions and Topics	To talk about the weather
	To use weather expressions
	To identify seasons
Linguistic Goals	To use *il fait* to talk about weather
Cultural Goals	To learn about climates in various regions of France

Block Schedule

Fun Break Using paper plates, have students divide their plates into 8 sections. They should decorate each section with a weather condition and a person wearing appropriate clothing. Then have them attach a spinner. Use the weather plates for practice and review. Students move the spinner and then describe what is happening on the spot where the spinner lands. ■

Day 1

Motivation and Focus

❑ Have students look at the map of France on page 4 and do the GEOGRAPHY ACTIVITY and PRE-VIEWING ACTIVITY, page 65 of the TE. Play the **Video** or read the **Videoscript** for section 4c.3 to introduce the climate of the different provinces, using the map on **Overhead Transparency** 1.

Presentation and Explanation

❑ *Lesson Opener:* Use the WARM-UP AND REVIEW activity on page 64 of the TE to practice months and dates. With books closed, act out or use **Video** or **Audio** CD 1, Tracks 46–47 to present the opening conversation. Ask students to read and summarize the conversation.

❑ *Pour communiquer:* Introduce and practice describing weather conditions with **Overhead Transparency** 13. Point out and have students repeat the expressions and names of the seasons in the *Pour communiquer* box, page 65.

Guided Practice and Checking Understanding

❑ Use **Overhead Visuals** Transparency 13 and the Activity on page A63 to practice weather expressions.
❑ Have students do the **Block Schedule Activity** at the top of this page.
❑ Use **Block Scheduling Copymasters** 25–32.
❑ To check understanding, use the **Audio** CD 6, Tracks 28–31 or read the **Audioscript** as students do **Workbook** Listening Activities A–D, pages 51–52.
❑ Play the **Video** or read the **Videoscript** and have students do **Video Activities** pages 111–113.
❑ Practice weather expressions using the COMPREHENSION activity on page 65 of the TE.

Independent Practice

❑ Have students do Activities 1 and 2 on page 65 individually and check their answers.
❑ Use any of the following activities for pair practice in talking about the weather: **Communipak** *Interview* 2, *Tu as la parole* 3 and 4, *Conversation* 3, *Échange* 2, or *Tête à tête* 2 (pages 133–149); or **Video Activities** page 114.
❑ Have students do any appropriate activities in **Activités pour tous,** pages 27–28.

Monitoring and Adjusting

❑ Assign **Workbook** Writing Activities 1–4, pages 53–54.
❑ Monitor students' use of weather expressions as they do the practice activities. Remind them to look at the *Pour communiquer* box on page 65 of the text as needed.

Reteaching (as needed)

❑ Have students redo any appropriate **Workbook** activities.
❑ Reteach weather expressions using **Teacher to Teacher**, page 6.
❑ Assign the **Video** for students who need to do review or makeup work.

Summary and Closure

❑ Show **Overhead Transparency** 1 and ask students to point out and talk about the climate of the regions of France that were studied in the lesson. Summarize information about the climate of French geographical regions and weather conditions.

Assessment

❑ Use Quiz 4 on pages 129–130 after students have completed the lesson. Use the **Test Generator** to adapt quiz questions to your class's needs.

Day 2

End-of-Unit Activities

Note: These activities may be done at the end of the unit, or at any time that seems appropriate during the unit.

❑ *À votre tour!:* Choose any or all of the Activities on pages 66–67. Students can use the **Audio** CD 1, Tracks 48–49 to check their responses for Activities 1 and 3. Arrange students in pairs/groups to practice and present the role plays in Activities 4–5. Activity 6 can be done as a whole-class activity. Use the CHALLENGE ACTIVITY on page 67 of the TE to practice using language from this and previous units.
❑ *Entracte 2:* Introduce parts of the body with the COMPREHENSION activity on page 68 of the TE. Read *Un jeu: Jacques a dit* on page 68 and play the game. You may also wish to play the GAME described in the margin on page 68 of the TE. Introduce the song *Alouette* with the PRE-READING activity on page 69 of the TE. Share the cultural note with the class, sing the song, and do the POST-READING activity.
❑ *Reading and Culture Activities:* Assign **Workbook** activities A–C, pages 55–57. Go over the answers with the class.

Day 3

Assessment

❑ Unit Test 2 (Form A or B) on pages 165–170 can be used as a comprehensive assessment of the unit's goals and objectives.
❑ Choose any or all of the **Performance Tests** as needed for additional assessment. The **Test Generator** can be used to modify test questions to meet your particular needs.

Nom _____

Classe _____ Date _____

Discovering
FRENCH
Nouveau!

BLEU

Unité 2
Leçon 4

Absent Student
Copymasters

LEÇON 4A L'heure, pages 56–59

Materials Checklist

- **Student Text**
- **Audio CD 1, Tracks 37–41; CD 6, Tracks 16–21**
- **Video 1 or DVD 1; Counter 56:47–1:05:09**
- **Workbook**

Steps to Follow

- Read *Un rendez-vous* on p. 56 in the text. Look at the photograph.
- Watch **Video** 1 or **DVD** 1; Counter 56:47–1:05:09, or listen to **Audio CD** 1, Tracks 37–38, 40–41.
- Read *Pour communiquer* (p. 56). Write the time indicated in the chart for each clock face.
- Do Activities 1 and 2 in the text (p. 57). Use **Audio CD** 1, Track 39. Write the parts for both speakers on a separate sheet of paper. Underline the time, for example, **Il est <u>quatre heures</u>**.
- Study how the French distinguish between A.M. and P.M. (p. 57).
- Study *Note de prononciation* (p. 57). Write out the times in the chart, underlining the liaisons. What letter is always silent?
- Read *À quelle heure est le film?* (p. 58).
- Study *Pour communiquer* (p. 58). Copy the expressions on a separate sheet of paper. Check the meanings.
- Do Activities 3, 4, 5, and 6 in the text (p. 59). For activities 4, 5, and 6 write the parts for both speakers. Write complete sentences for all answers on a separate sheet.
- Do **Writing Activities** 1, 2, 3 in the **Workbook** (pp. 43–44).
- Do **Listening Activities** A–F in the **Workbook** (pp. 41–42). Use **Audio CD** 6, Tracks 16–21.

If You Don't Understand . . .

- Watch the **Video** or **DVD** in a quiet place. Try to stay focused. If you get lost, stop the **Video** or **DVD**. Replay it and find your place.
- Listen to the **CDs** in a quiet place. Try to stay focused. If you get lost, stop the **CDs**. Replay them and find your place.
- Repeat aloud with the audio. Try to sound like the people on the recording.
- On a separate sheet of paper, write down the words that are new. Check for meaning.
- Say aloud anything you write. Make sure you understand everything you say.
- Write down any questions so that you can ask your partner or your teacher later.

Nom _____

Classe _____ Date _____

Unité 2
Leçon 4

Absent Student
Copymasters

Discovering
FRENCH
Nouveau!

BLEU

Self-Check

Write out the times for each of the following events. Be precise about whether the event takes place in the morning, the afternoon, or the evening. Write complete sentences on a separate sheet of paper.

1. film / 7h du soir
2. rendez-vous / 10h20 du matin
3. train pour Paris / 7h15 du soir
4. le déjeuner / 1h de l'après-midi
5. le match de football / 2h30 de l'après-midi

Nom _____

Classe _____ Date _____ _____

Discovering
FRENCH
Nouveau!

BLEU

Unité 2
Leçon 4

Absent Student
Copymasters

LEÇON 4B Le jour et la date, pages 60–63

Materials Checklist

- **Student Text**
- **Audio CD 1, Tracks 42–45; CD 6, Tracks 22–27**
- **Video 1** or **DVD 1; Counter 1:06:24–1:11:09**
- **Workbook**

Steps to Follow

- Read *Quel jour est-ce?* (p. 60). Look at the pictures.
- Watch **Video** 1 or **DVD** 1; Counter 1:06:24–1:11:09, or listen to **Audio CD** 1, Tracks 42–45.
- Read *Pour communiquer* (p. 61). Write the words and expressions several times on a separate sheet of paper.
- Do Activity 1 in the text (p. 61). Answer in complete sentences.
- Do Activities 2 and 3 in the text (p. 61). On a separate sheet of paper, write the parts for both speakers. Underline the names of the days of the week in each sentence.
- Read *Anniversaire* (p. 62*)*.
- Study *Pour communiquer* (p. 62). Write the new expressions several times on a separate sheet of paper.
- Do Activity 6 in the text (p. 63). Write complete sentences on a separate sheet of paper. Underline the expressions for the dates in each answer, for example, **C'est le quinze septembre**.
- Do **Writing Activities** 1, 2, 3, 4 in the **Workbook** (pp. 48–49).
- Do **Listening Activities** A–F in the **Workbook** (pp. 45–47). Use **Audio CD** 6, Tracks 22–27.

If You Don't Understand . . .

- Reread activity directions. Put the directions in your own words.
- When writing a sentence, ask yourself, "What do I mean? What am I trying to say?"
- Watch the **Video** or **DVD** in a quiet place. Try to stay focused. If you get lost, stop the **Video** or **DVD**. Replay it and find your place.
- Listen to the **CDs** in a quiet place. Try to stay focused. If you get lost, stop the **CDs**. Replay them and find your place.
- Repeat aloud with the audio. Try to sound like the people on the recording.
- On a separate sheet of paper, write down the words that are new. Check for meaning.
- Say aloud anything you write. Make sure you understand everything you say.
- Write down any questions so that you can ask your partner or your teacher later.

Self-Check

What is the date? Write the following dates in complete sentences. Underline the date in each sentence.

1. 14 juillet
2. 13 janvier
3. 12 octobre
4. 4 juin
5. 10 novembre
6. 8 avril

Answers

Nom _____

Classe _____ Date _____

Discovering
FRENCH
Nouveau!

B L E U

LEÇON 4C Le temps, pages 64–65

Materials Checklist

- **Student Text**
- **Audio CD** 1, Tracks 46–49; **CD** 6, Tracks 28–31
- **Video** 1 or **DVD** 1; Counter 1:11:30–1:16:50
- **Workbook**

Steps to Follow

- Read *Le temps* (p. 64). Look at the facial expressions of Cécile and her brother Philippe and read the captions.
- Watch **Video** 1 or **DVD** 1; Counter 1:11:30–1:16:50, or listen to **Audio CD** 1, Tracks 46–47.
- Read *Pour communiquer* (p. 65). Copy the new expressions on a separate sheet of paper. Copy the chart, *Les saisons*, and check the meanings.
- Do Activities 1 and 2 in the text (p. 65). Write your answers in complete sentences on a separate sheet of paper.
- Do **Writing Activities** 1, 2, 3, 4 in the **Workbook** (pp. 53–54).
- Do **Listening Activities** A–D in the **Workbook** (pp. 51–52). Use **Audio CD** 6, Tracks 28–31.
- Do Activities 1–6 of *À votre tour!* in the text (pp. 66–67). Use **Audio CD** 1, Tracks 48–49 with Activities 1 and 3.

If You Don't Understand . . .

- Reread activity directions. Put the directions in your own words.
- Say aloud everything that you write. Be sure you understand what you are saying.
- Write down questions so that you can ask your partner or your teacher later.
- When writing a sentence, ask yourself, "What do I mean? What am I trying to say?"
- Watch the **Video** or **DVD** in a quiet place. Try to stay focused. If you get lost, stop the **Video** or **DVD**. Replay it and find your place in the text.
- Listen to the **CDs** in a quiet place. Try to stay focused. If you get lost, stop the **CDs**. Replay them and find your place in the text.
- Listen once without repeating. Then replay and repeat aloud with the audio. Try to sound like the people on the recording. Imitate their sounds and accents. Pause the **CD** if you can't keep up.

Self-Check

Review the expressions using the seasons. Write complete sentences saying what Anne likes to do in each of the seasons indicated.

1. le printemps / jouer au tennis
2. l'été / nager
3. l'automne / faire des promenades
4. l'hiver / faire du ski
5. le printemps / jouer au baseball
6. l'été / voyager

Answers

1. Au printemps, elle aime jouer au tennis.   2. En été, elle aime nager.   3. En automne, elle aime faire des promenades.   4. En hiver, elle aime faire du ski.   5. Au printemps, elle aime jouer au baseball.   6. En été, elle aime voyager.

Nom _____

Classe _____ Date _____

Discovering
FRENCH
Nouveau!

BLEU

Unité 2
Leçon 4

Family Involvement

LEÇON 4 De jour en jour

Les jours de la semaine

Ask a family member what day it is today. Use the calendar below to determine the day.
Explain that in the French-speaking world, Monday is the first day of the week.

- First, explain your assignment.
- Then, ask the question, **Quel jour est-ce aujourd'hui?**
- Help him or her pronounce the words correctly by modeling the pronunciation of the days
  of the week. Point to the word as you model the pronunciation.
- After you get the answer, complete the sentence at the bottom of the page.

LUNDI	MARDI	MERCREDI	JEUDI	VENDREDI	SAMEDI	DIMANCHE
					1	2
3	4	5	6	7	8	9
10	11	12	13	14	15	16
17	18	19	20	21	22	23
24 / 31	25	26	27	28	29	30

Aujourd'hui, c'est _____.

Nom _____

Classe _____ Date _____

Joyeux anniversaire!

Ask a family member to identify the months in which different family members have birthdays.

- First, explain your assignment.
- Next, help him or her pronounce the months of the year correctly by modeling the pronunciation. Point to each word as you model the answers.
- Then, model his or her statement by saying when one of your family members has a birthday.

Modèle: **L'anniversaire de John est en avril.**

After you get the information on three family members, complete the sentences at the bottom of the page.

Les mois de l'année *(Months of the year)*

janvier	avril	juillet	octobre
février	mai	août	novembre
mars	juin	septembre	décembre

L'anniversaire de _____ est en _____.

L'anniversaire de _____ est en _____.

L'anniversaire de _____ est en _____.

Nom _____

Classe _____ Date _____ _____

Discovering FRENCH *Nouveau!*

B L E U

Unité 2
Leçon 4

Video Activities

MODULE 4A L'heure

Video 1, DVD 1

 4a.1 Activité 1. Un rendez-vous

As you watch and listen to the conversation between Stéphanie and Jean-Paul, put a check mark in front of the sentence that is said *first* in each exchange.

1. _____ Quelle heure est-il? _____ Il est trois heures.

2. _____ Trois heures? _____ Oui, trois heures.

3. _____ Au revoir, Stéphanie. À bientôt. _____ Oh là là! J'ai un rendez-vous avec David dans vingt minutes. Au revoir, Jean-Paul.

4a.2 Activité 2. L'heure

What time do the people in the video say it is? As each person says a time, draw a line from that person's name to the appropriate clock.

1. Papa `12:00`

2. Frédéric `1:00`

3. Trinh `2:00`

4. Monsieur Masson `6:00`

5. Madame Chollet `8:00`

6. Monsieur Saint-Louis `11:00`

7. Mademoiselle Lacour `10:00`

Nom _____

Classe _____ Date _____

4a.2 Activité 3. L'heure exacte

Listen to the people in the video as they give the exact time in French. Then fill in the minute hand in each clock below.

▶—Il est une heure et quart.

a. 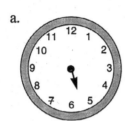 b. 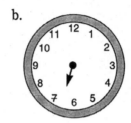 c. 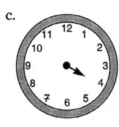 d.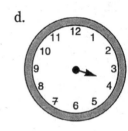

4a.3 Activité 4. Dialogue: À quelle heure est le film?

Counter 1:01:41–1:02:00

Listen to the conversation between Stéphanie and David. Then, using words from the box below, fill in the cartoon bubbles with the time David gives.

et quart   et demie   moins le quart

1. —Quelle heure est-il?

   Il est trois heures _____.

2. —Et à quelle heure est le film?

   À quatre heures _____.

Nom _____

Classe _____ Date _____

Discovering
FRENCH *Nouveau!*

B L E U

Unité 2
Leçon 4
Video Activities

4a.4 Activité 5. À quelle heure?

At what time are the events below taking place? Watch the video to find out and draw a line from each event to the corresponding time it is taking place. (*Note:* One time is not used.)

1. la classe de français   a. 2 h 15

2. le dîner   b. 5 h 45

3. le film   c. 7 h 30

4. le train de Toulouse   d. 9 h 10

5. le bus   e. 11 h 00

                                   f. 1 h 50

4a.5 Activité 6. L'heure officielle

Watch the **Vignette culturelle** to learn about official time in France. Then give the equivalents for the following times, using the twenty-four hour system.

▶ 1 h 00 de l'après-midi   13 h 00

1. 2 h 25 de l'après-midi   _____

2. 10 h 45 du soir   _____

3. 12 h 00 du soir   _____

4. 4 h 15 de l'après-midi   _____

5. 6 h 30 du soir   _____

6. 8 h 10 du soir   _____

Question d'opinion: Should the United States adopt official time for schedules and listings? Why or why not?

Réponse: _____

_____

Nom _____

Classe _____ Date _____

B L E U

 Activité 7. Le train

Now that you have learned about the use of official time in France, look at the train schedule. With a partner, play the roles of a tourist asking at what time certain trains leave and an employee at the train station answering the questions based on the schedule. Alternate roles with your partner. Follow the model.

▶   TOURIST: **À quelle heure est le train de Cannes?**

    EMPLOYEE: **Le train de Cannes est à quinze heures dix.**

Orange	10.30
Avignon	11.50
Arles	13.05
Cannes	15.10
Antibes	18.45
Nice	22.30

Nom _____

Classe _____ Date _____

Unité 2
Leçon 4
Video Activities

Discovering
FRENCH *Nouveau!*

B L E U

MODULE 4B   Quel jour est-ce?

Video 1, DVD 1

4b.1 Activité 1. Dialogues: A. Quel jour est-ce?
(What day is it?)

Counter 1:06:24–1:06:41

Watch the video and fill in the missing day in
the cartoon bubbles below.

mercredi	samedi	dimanche	jeudi	vendredi

1.

Quel jour est-ce?

C'est _____ .

Super! Demain, c'est
_____ !

2.

Aujourd'hui, c'est
_____ .

Et alors?

Demain, c'est
_____

Le jour de l'examen.

Zut! C'est vrai!

URB
p. 107

Nom _____

Classe _____ Date _____

Discovering
FRENCH
Nouveau!

BLEU

4b.1 Activité 2. B. Deux anniversaires

Isabelle and François both have birthdays in March. As they tell you the dates, write the numbers in the calendar pads below.

1.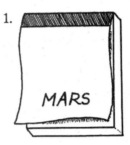

MARS

Isabelle

2.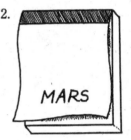

MARS

François

Quelle coïncidence!

4b.2 Activité 3. Quelle est la date?

Counter 1:06:42–1:09:20

As the people in the video say the date, draw a line from the day on the left to the corresponding month on the right. The dates are given in the order they appear in the video. Some months will be used more than once.

1. le deux   juillet

2. le trente   juin

3. le premier   septembre

4. le quinze   février

5. le vingt-quatre   novembre

6. le premier   mars

7. le huit   août

8. le trois   avril

9. le quatre   mai

10. le vingt-deux

11. le trois

Nom _____

Classe _____ Date _____

**Discovering
FRENCH**
Nouveau!

BLEU

Unité 2
Leçon 4

Video Activities

4b.2 Activité 4. C'est quand, votre anniversaire?

When do the people in the video celebrate their birthdays? Write the missing month in the birthday cakes below. The first one has been done for you.

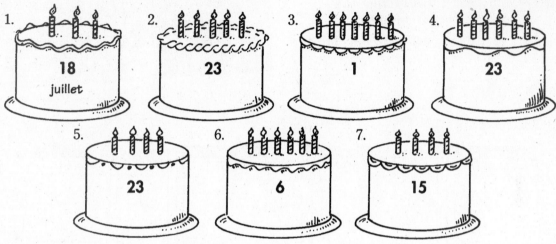

1. **18** juillet
2. **23**
3. **1**
4. **23**
5. **23**
6. **6**
7. **15**

 ## 4b.3 Activité 5. Joyeux anniversaire!

Counter 1:09:21–1:11:09

A. How do you celebrate your birthday? Before you watch the **Vignette culturelle**, write a brief description of a typical birthday celebration below.

Mon anniversaire: _____

_____

B. Now watch the **Vignette culturelle**. Then answer the questions below.

1. What is **le gâteau d'anniversaire?** _____

2. What is the equivalent of **Joyeux anniversaire** in English? _____

C. Question personnelle: How does your birthday celebration differ from Philippe's?

Réponse: _____

_____

Nom _____

Classe _____ Date _____

 Activité 6. C'est quand, ton anniversaire?

Now that you have learned to say the date in French, interview your classmates to find out their birthdays. Record each date under the appropriate month in the calendars below. Answer your classmates when they ask you when your birthday is. Follow the model.

▶   TOI: **C'est quand, ton anniversaire?**

UN/UNE CAMARADE: **C'est le 23 décembre.**

 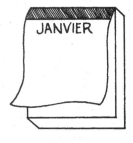  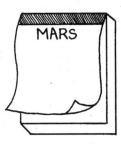 

JANVIER   FÉVRIER   MARS   AVRIL

MAI   JUIN   JUILLET   AOÛT

SEPTEMBRE   OCTOBRE   NOVEMBRE   DÉCEMBRE

Nom _____

Classe _____ Date _____

Discovering
FRENCH
Nouveau!

B L E U

Unité 2
Leçon 4

Video Activities

MODULE 4C Le temps

Video 1, DVD 1

4c.1 Activité 1. Dialogue: Le temps

Counter 1:11:30–1:12:10

Watch as Philippe and Cécile discuss the weather and their plans for the day. Then mark an **X** before the sentences you hear below.

1. _____ Il fait froid!

   _____ Il fait mauvais!

2. _____ Il neige.

   _____ Il pleut.

3. _____ Papa va nous inviter au restaurant.

   _____ Papa va nous inviter au cinéma.

4c.2 Activité 2. La date et le temps

Counter 1:12:11–1:13:53

Listen and watch as people talk about the weather in France. For each date mentioned, put a check mark under the weather expression that describes that day.

| | Il fait . . . | | | | | | Il . . . | |
	chaud	beau	bon	frais	mauvais	froid	pleut	neige
1. 12 janvier								
2. 3 février								
3. 8 mars								
4. 1 avril								
5. 13 juin								
6. 20 juillet								
7. 2 octobre								
8. 24 novembre								
9. 17 décembre								

Nom _____

Classe _____ Date _____

4c.3 Activité 3. La géographie de la France

As you watch the **Vignette culturelle**, decide whether each statement below is true **(vrai)** or false **(faux)**. Then mark an **X** in the box in the appropriate column.

	vrai	faux
1. Geographically, France is a very diverse country.	❑	❑
2. The Pyrenees mountains border France to the east.	❑	❑
3. **Le Massif Central** are mountains in the center of France.	❑	❑
4. France is bordered to the south by the Mediterranean.	❑	❑
5. **La Touraine** is located in northern France along the Seine River.	❑	❑
6. With its many flower gardens, Touraine is called **le Jardin de la France**.	❑	❑
7. French kings built their castles in Touraine.	❑	❑
8. The province of Alsace has a mild climate.	❑	❑
9. Many people in Alsace speak **l'alsacien**, a dialect of French.	❑	❑
10. **La Savoie** is a province located in the Vosges mountains.	❑	❑
11. Every winter millions of French people come to **la Savoie** to enjoy skiing.	❑	❑
12. France's Mediterranean coast is known as **la Côte d'Azur**, or the French Riviera.	❑	❑
13. People from around the world come to Nice for the annual film festival.	❑	❑

Discovering FRENCH *Nouveau!*

BLEU

 4c.3 Activité 4. Bonjour, la France!

After learning about the geography of France in the **Vignette culturelle**, write the names of the mountain ranges and regions from the box in the appropriate blanks on the map.

les montagnes	les régions
les Alpes	l'Alsace
le Massif Central	la Provence
les Pyrénées	la Savoie
les Vosges	la Touraine

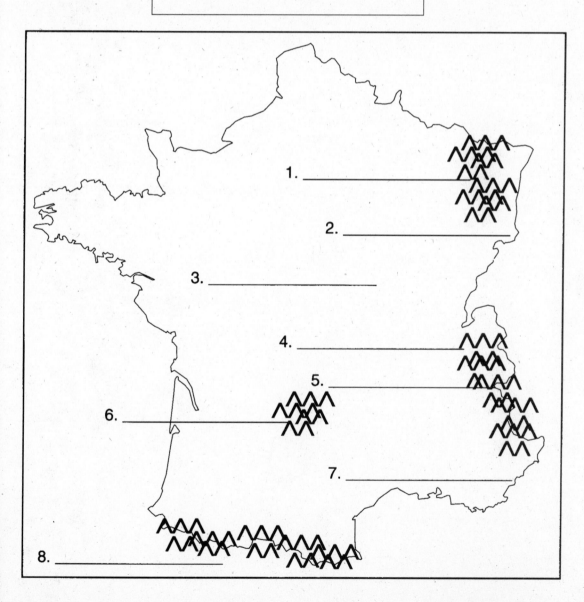

1. _____

2. _____

3. _____

4. _____

5. _____

6. _____

7. _____

8. _____

Nom _____

Classe _____ Date _____

Discovering
FRENCH
Nouveau

B L E U

Activité 5. Quel temps fait-il?

Look at the weather map below. Now that you know some weather expressions, take turns with a partner asking what the weather is like in one of the cities shown on the map. Follow the model.

Il fait chaud	Il fait bon	Il fait beau	Il fait frais
Il pleut	Il fait mauvais	Il fait froid	Il neige

▶   ÉLÈVE 1: **Quel temps fait-il à Strasbourg?**
      ÉLÈVE 2: **Il pleut. (Il fait mauvais.)**

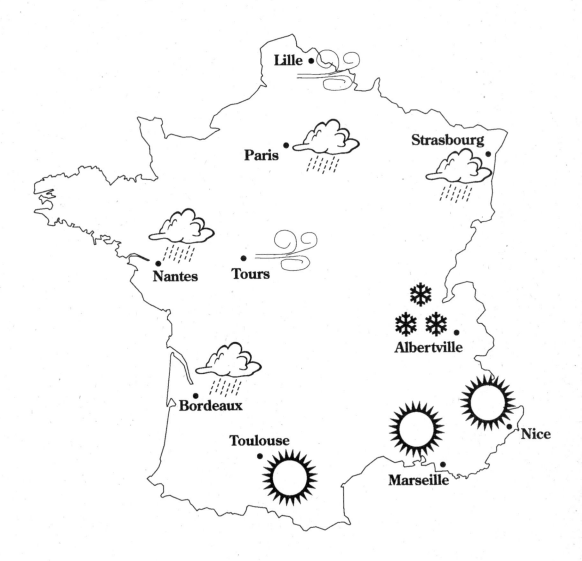

Discovering
FRENCH
Nouveau!

B L E U

Unité 2
Leçon 4

Videoscripts

MODULE 4A   L'heure

Video 1, DVD 1

4a.1 Dialogue: Un rendez-vous

Counter 56:47–57:13

Jean-Paul and Stéphanie are at a café. Stéphanie is in a hurry to leave. Let's listen and find out why.

STÉPHANIE: Quelle heure est-il?
JEAN-PAUL: Il est trois heures.
STÉPHANIE: Trois heures?
JEAN-PAUL: Oui, trois heures.
STÉPHANIE: Oh là là! J'ai un rendez-vous avec David dans vingt minutes. Au revoir, Jean-Paul.
JEAN-PAUL: Au revoir, Stéphanie. À bientôt!

4a.2 Mini-scenes: Telling time

Counter 57:17–1:01:40

Did you notice how Stéphanie asked Jean-Paul the time? Watch again.

STÉPHANIE: Quelle heure est-il?
JEAN-PAUL: Il est trois heures.

In France, as in the United States, people like to be on time . . . so it's important to know what time it is. Watch these scenes.

—Dis, Papa. Quelle heure est-il?
—Il est six heures.

—Dis, Frédéric. Quelle heure est-il?
—Il est huit heures.

—Dis, Trinh. Quelle heure est-il? . . . Quelle heure est-il?
—Il est une heure.
—Merci.

—Pardon, monsieur. Quelle heure est-il?
—Il est midi.

—Pardon, madame. Quelle heure est-il?
—Il est onze heures.
—Merci.

—Pardon, monsieur. Quelle heure est-il?
—Il est dix heures.

—Pardon, mademoiselle. Quelle heure est-il?
—Il est deux heures.
—Merci.

Now it's your turn to tell the time. Watch the scenes. For each scene, say what time it is.

—Quelle heure est-il? [screen card]
—Il est huit heures.

—Quelle heure est-il? [screen card]
—Il est dix heures.

—Quelle heure est-il? [screen card]
—Il est midi.

—Quelle heure est-il? [screen card]
—Il est une heure.

—Quelle heure est-il? [screen card]
—Il est trois heures.

—Quelle heure est-il? [screen card]
—Il est quatre heures.

—Quelle heure est-il? [screen card]
—Il est neuf heures.

—Quelle heure est-il? [screen card]
—Il est minuit.

*To give the quarter hours and the half hour, French people use the expressions **et quart**, **et demie**, and **moins le quart**. To indicate the minutes, they say the number of minutes after the hour. Watch these scenes.*

—Quelle heure est-il?
—Il est une heure et quart.

—Quelle heure est-il?
—Il est cinq heures et demie.
—Merci.

—Quelle heure est-il?
—Il est sept heures moins le quart.

—Pardon, monsieur. Quelle heure est-il?
—Il est quatre heures cinq.

—Quelle heure est-il?
—Il est trois heures cinquante.

It's your turn again to tell the time. Watch the scenes and say what time it is.

—Quelle heure est-il? [screen card]
—Il est huit heures et quart.

—Quelle heure est-il? [screen card]
—Il est dix heures et quart.

—Quelle heure est-il? [screen card]
—Il est onze heures et demie.

Unité 2
Leçon 4

Videoscripts

Discovering
FRENCH *Nouveau!*

BLEU

—Quelle heure est-il? [screen card]
—Il est deux heures moins le quart.

—Quelle heure est-il? [screen card]
—Il est six heures dix.

—Quelle heure est-il? [screen card]
—Il est neuf heures vingt.

—Quelle heure est-il? [screen card]
—Il est dix heures quarante.

4a.3 À quelle heure est le film?

Counter 1:01:41–1:02:00

Stéphanie is rushing to meet David. They are planning to go to a movie. Listen!

STÉPHANIE: Quelle heure est-il?
DAVID: Il est trois heures et demie.
STÉPHANIE: Et à quelle heure est le film?
DAVID: À quatre heures et quart.
STÉPHANIE: Ça va. Nous avons le temps.

Did you notice how Stéphanie asked David what time the movie was? Watch again.

STÉPHANIE: Et à quelle heure est le film?
DAVID: À quatre heures et quart.

4a.4 Mini-scenes: Indicating at what time an event occurs

Counter 1:02:01–1:02:37

Now watch these scenes.

—Dis, Marc, à quelle heure est la classe de français?
—À onze heures.

—Dis, Maman, à quelle heure est le dîner?
—À sept heures et demie.

—Dis, Anne, à quelle heure est le film?
—À neuf heures dix.

—Pardon, madame, à quelle heure est le train de Toulouse?
—À six heures moins le quart.
—Merci.

—Pardon monsieur (madame), à quelle heure est le bus?
—À deux heures moins dix.
—Merci.

4a.5 Vignette culturelle: L'heure officielle

Counter 1:02:38–1:05:09

How do you distinguish between morning and afternoon hours in English? Simply by
adding A.M. or P.M. to the time. Similarly, French people differentiate between the various periods of the day by using the expressions:

> **du matin**
> **de l'après-midi**
> **du soir**

The French also have an official way of telling time which they use on train schedules and TV listings. In this system, the day is divided into 24 hours.

For the 24-hour clock, the hours from 0 up to 12 correspond to A.M., while the hours from 12 to 24 correspond to P.M. To figure out the afternoon hours, you simply add 12.

Let's see how the system works:

> *1 P.M. becomes 13 hours.* **Il est treize heures.**
>
> *3 P.M. becomes 15 hours.* **Il est quinze heures.**
>
> *8 P.M. becomes 20 hours.* **Il est vingt heures.**

Of course, if someone tells you the official time, and you want to figure out the corresponding American time, you simply subtract 12.

For example, **seize heures**, *16 hours, becomes 4 P.M.* **Vingt-deux heures**, *22 hours, becomes 10 P.M.*

Now let's see the complete 24-hour clock.

Now watch the following scenes and try to understand the times.

—Pardon, monsieur. Quelle heure est il?
—Il est dix-sept heures.
—Merci.

—Pardon, monsieur, à quelle heure est le train de Nice?
—À dix-neuf heures quarante-sept.
—Merci

—Pardon, madame. Quelle heure est il?
—Dix-huit heures vingt.
—Merci.

—S'il vous plaît, à quelle heure est le film?
—À vingt et une heures, mademoiselle.
—Merci beaucoup.

MODULE 4B Quel jour est-ce?

Video 1, DVD 1
4b.1 Dialogues:
A. Quel jour est-ce?

Counter 1:06:24–1:06:41

What is your favorite day of the week? For many people, the days of the week are not all alike!

PHILLIPE: Quel jour est-ce?
STÉPHANIE: C'est vendredi!
PHILIPPE: Super! Demain, c'est samedi!

NATHALIE: Ça va?
MARC: Pas très bien.
NATHALIE: Pourquoi?
MARC: Aujourd'hui, c'est mercredi.
NATHALIE: Et alors?
MARC: Demain, c'est jeudi! Le jour de l'examen.
NATHALIE: Zut! C'est vrai! Au revoir, Marc.
MARC: Au revoir, Nathalie. À demain!

B. Anniversaire

François and Isabelle are on their way to a birthday party. They're talking about their own birthdays. Listen.

FRANÇOIS: C'est quand, ton anniversaire?
ISABELLE: C'est le 18 mars!
FRANÇOIS: Le 18 mars? Pas possible!
ISABELLE: Si! Pourquoi?
FRANÇOIS: C'est aussi mon anniversaire.
ISABELLE: Quelle coïncidence!

4b.2 Mini-scenes: Dates and birthdays

Counter 1:06:42–1:09:20

Did you notice how Isabelle told François the date of her birthday? Listen again.

FRANÇOIS: C'est quand, ton anniversaire?
ISABELLE: C'est le 18 mars!

To give a date, French people use the construction: le plus the number plus the name of the month.

le 18 janvier
le 3 décembre
le premier avril

Let's ask a few people what day it is today.

Quel jour est-ce aujourd'hui?

—C'est le trente mars.

—C'est le premier juin.

—C'est le quinze avril.

—C'est le vingt-quatre mai.

—C'est le deux février.

—C'est le vingt-deux mars.

—C'est le trois juin.

—C'est le premier juillet.

—C'est le sept août.
—Mais non, c'est le huit août.
—Ah oui, c'est vrai. C'est le huit août.

—C'est le trois septembre.
—C'est vrai. C'est le trois septembre.

—C'est le quatre novembre.

Now it's your turn to give the date. As you watch the following scenes, say what day it is.

—Quel jour est-ce?   [screen card]
—C'est le 5 décembre.

—Quel jour est-ce?   [C'est le 26 avril.]

—Quel jour est-ce?   [C'est le 16 août.]

—Quel jour est-ce?   [C'est le 14 mai.]

—Quel jour est-ce?   [C'est le 21 juillet.]

—Quel jour est-ce?   [C'est le 12 septembre.]

—Quel jour est-ce?   [C'est le premier octobre.]

—Quel jour est-ce?   [C'est le 30 janvier.]

Let's ask these people when their birthdays are.

C'est quand, votre anniversaire?

—C'est le 18 juillet.
—C'est le 23 décembre.
—Moi, c'est le premier mars.

BLEU

—Et moi, c'est le 23 mai.
—Tiens, moi aussi, c'est le 23 mai.

—C'est le 6 novembre.
—Moi, c'est le 15 janvier.

4b.3 Vignette culturelle: Joyeux anniversaire! Counter 1:09:21–1:11:09

Have you been to a birthday party lately? French teenagers celebrate birthdays pretty much like Americans.

—Salut!
—Salut!
—Bon anniversaire!
—Merci!
—Salut!
—Merci.

Guests bring presents to the friend who is having the birthday.

—Bonjour!
—Salut!
—Tiens, c'est pour toi.
—Merci. Qu'est-ce que c'est?
—Regarde!
—. . . Ah, merci, un compact! . . . Ah, merci, un Astérix!

*After the presents have been opened, there's the birthday cake: **le gâteau d'anniversaire**. Everyone sings "Happy Birthday," in French of course!*

Joyeux anniversaire . . . Joyeux anniversaire . . .

—Vous voulez du gâteau? Il est délicieux!

Discovering
FRENCH
Nouveau!

BLEU

Unité 2
Leçon 4

Videoscripts

MODULE 4C   Le temps

Video 1, DVD 1

4c.1 Dialogue: Le temps
Counter 1:11:30–1:12:10

Has it ever happened to you that on the day you had planned a picnic, the weather turned out to be miserable? It happened to Cécile. Watch! It's eight o'clock Sunday morning.

CÉCILE: Quel temps fait-il?
PHILIPPE: Il fait mauvais!
CÉCILE: Il fait mauvais?
PHILIPPE: Oui, il fait mauvais! Regarde! Il pleut!
CÉCILE: Oh, zut, zut et zut! . . . Et le pique-nique?
PHILIPPE: Le pique-nique? Ah, oui, le pique-nique! . . . Écoute, ça n'a pas d'importance.
CÉCILE: Pourquoi?
PHILIPPE: Pourquoi? Parce que Papa va nous inviter au restaurant.
CÉCILE: Super!

4c.2 Mini-scenes: Talking about weather
Counter 1:12:11–1:13:53

In France, as in the United States, everyone likes to talk about the weather. Listen.

—C'est le 12 janvier. Il neige

—C'est le 3 février. Il fait froid.

—C'est le 8 mars. Il fait frais aujourd'hui.

—C'est le premier avril.
—Quel temps fait-il?
—Il pleut.

—C'est 13 juin.
—Quel temps fait-il aujourd'hui?
—Il fait bon.

—C'est le 20 juillet.
—Quel temps fait-il aujourd'hui?
—Il fait chaud.

—C'est le 2 octobre.
—Quel temps fait-il?
—Il pleut.

—C'est le 24 novembre.
—Quel temps fait-il?
—Il fait mauvais.

—C'est le 17 décembre.
—Quel temps fait-il?
—Il fait froid.

Now it's your turn to talk about the weather. Look at the cartoons and describe the weather.

—Quel temps fait-il?   [screen card]
—Il fait chaud.

—Quel temps fait-il?   [screen card]
—Il fait froid.

—Quel temps fait-il?   [screen card]
—Il fait beau.

—Quel temps fait-il?   [screen card]
—Il fait mauvais.

—Quel temps fait-il?   [screen card]
—Il pleut.

—Quel temps fait-il?   [screen card]
—Il neige.

4c.3 Vignette culturelle: La géographie de la France
Counter 1:13:54–1:16:50

*Geographically, France is a very diverse country. It has plains in the east and the west. It has high mountains on its borders: the Alps, **les Alpes**, in the east and the Pyrenees, **les Pyrénées**, in the south. It also has smaller mountains in the northeast, **les Vosges**, and in the center of the country, **le Massif Central**. France has a very long coastline. It's bordered by the Atlantic Ocean, **l'océan Atlantique**, on the west, and the Mediterranean, **la Méditerranée**, on the south. The French provinces each have a character of their own. Let's visit some of them.*

*The province of Touraine, **la Touraine**, is located in central France along the Loire River. It has a gentle climate, with mild winters and warm summers. Because of*

this climate, **la Touraine** has magnificent flower gardens. In fact, the province is called **le Jardin de la France**, the Garden of France. It is in Touraine that the kings of France built their castles. This is the castle of Amboise.

Here is the castle of Chenonceau.

This is the castle of Chambord.

Many people say that the purest French is spoken in Touraine.

The province of Alsace, **l'Alsace**, is situated along the Vosges mountains. It has a continental climate with cold winters and warm summers. Alsace is located across the Rhine River from Germany. In many Alsatian villages, people still speak a dialect of German called Alsatian, **l'alsacien**.

Now let's go south to **la Savoie**. This province is located in the Alps, across the border from Switzerland and Italy. **La Savoie** is known for its many ski resorts. Every winter millions of French people come to enjoy their favorite sport.

Now, let's visit **Provence**. The Mediterranean coast is known as the French Riviera, **la côte d'Azur**. Located in the south of France, **Provence** and **la côte d'Azur** have a very mild climate. In winter, it's fairly warm, and in summer the weather is beautiful. Every year millions of tourists come to enjoy the sun and the many water sports. In May, movie stars and directors from around the world come to Cannes for the annual film festival.

France is very beautiful, isn't it?

LEÇON 4   De jour en jour

PE AUDIO

Vidéo-scène A. L'heure

CD 1, Track 37

Compréhension orale
Listening Comprehension

1. Un rendez-vous, p. 56

Jean-Paul and Stéphanie are sitting in a café. Stéphanie seems to be in a hurry to leave.

STÉPHANIE: Quelle heure est-il?
JEAN-PAUL: Il est trois heures.
STÉPHANIE: Trois heures?
JEAN-PAUL: Oui, trois heures.
STÉPHANIE: Oh là là. J'ai un rendez-vous avec David dans vingt minutes. Au revoir, Jean-Paul.
JEAN-PAUL: Au revoir, Stéphanie. À bientôt!

CD 1, Track 38

Écoutez et répétez. Listen and repeat. **p. 56**

You will now hear a paused version of the dialog. Listen to the speaker and repeat right after he or she has completed the sentence.

CD 1, Track 39

1. Écoutez bien! p. 57

Listen as people talk about the time. For each dialog, indicate which of the watches below corresponds to the time you hear.

1. —Quelle heure est-il?
   —Il est sept heures. #

2. —Quelle heure est-il?
   —Il est deux heures. #

3. —Quelle heure est-il?
   —Il est huit heures. #

4. —Quelle heure est-il?
   —Il est midi. #

5. —Quelle heure est-il?
   —Il est dix heures. #

6. —Quelle heure est-il?
   —Il est cinq heures. #

CD 1, Track 40

Compréhension orale
Listening Comprehension

2. À quelle heure est le film? p. 58

Stéphanie and David have decided to go to a movie.

STÉPHANIE: Quelle heure est-il?
DAVID: Il est trois heures et demie.
STÉPHANIE: Et à quelle heure est le film?
DAVID: À quatre heures et quart.
STÉPHANIE: Ça va. Nous avons le temps.

CD 1, Track 41

Écoutez et répétez. Listen and repeat. **p. 58**

You will now hear a paused version of the dialog. Listen to the speaker and repeat after he or she has completed the sentence.

Vidéo-scène B. Le jour et la date

CD 1, Track 42

1. Quel jour est-ce? p. 60

Compréhension orale
Listening Comprehension

For many people, the days of the week are not all alike.

Dialogue 1. Vendredi

PHILIPPE: Quel jour est-ce?
STÉPHANIE: C'est vendredi!
PHILIPPE: Super! Demain, c'est samedi!

Dialogue 2. Mercredi

NATHALIE: Ça va?
MARC: Pas très bien.
NATHALIE: Pourquoi?
MARC: Aujourd'hui, c'est mercredi.
NATHALIE: Et alors?
MARC: Demain, c'est jeudi! Le jour de l'examen.
NATHALIE: Zut! C'est vrai! Au revoir, Marc.
MARC: Au revoir, Nathalie. À demain!

Unité 2
Leçon 4

Audioscripts

Discovering
FRENCH
Nouveau!

BLEU

CD 1, Track 43

Écoutez et répétez. Listen and repeat. p. 60

You will now hear a paused version of the dialogue. Listen to the speaker and repeat right after he or she has completed the sentence.

CD 1, Track 44

2. Anniversaire, p. 62

C. Compréhension orale
Listening Comprehension

François and Isabelle are on their way to Nathalie's birthday party. As they are talking, François wants to know when Isabelle's birthday is.

FRANÇOIS: C'est quand, ton anniversaire?
ISABELLE: C'est le 18 mars!
FRANÇOIS: Le 18 mars? Pas possible!
ISABELLE: Si! Pourquoi?
FRANÇOIS: C'est aussi mon anniversaire.
ISABELLE: Quelle coïncidence!

CD 1, Track 45

Écoutez et répétez. Listen and repeat. p. 62

You will now hear a paused version of the dialogue. Listen to the speaker and repeat right after he or she has completed the sentence.

Vidéo-scène C. Le temps

CD 1, Track 46

A. Compréhension orale
Listening Comprehension

Quel temps fait-il? p. 64

It is nine o'clock Sunday morning. Cécile and her brother Philippe have planned a picnic for the whole family. Cécile is asking about the weather.

CÉCILE: Quel temps fait-il?
PHILIPPE: Il fait mauvais!
CÉCILE: Il fait mauvais?
PHILIPPE: Oui, il fait mauvais! Regarde! Il pleut!
CÉCILE: Zut, zut, et zut!
PHILIPPE: !!!???

CÉCILE: Et le pique-nique?
PHILIPPE: Ah, oui, le pique-nique! . . . Écoute, ça n'a pas d'importance.
CÉCILE: Pourquoi?
PHILIPPE: Pourquoi? Parce que Papa va nous inviter au restaurant.
CÉCILE: Super!

CD 1, Track 47

Écoutez et répétez. Listen and repeat. p. 64

You will now hear a paused version of the dialogue. Listen to the speaker and repeat right after he or she has completed the sentence.

À votre tour!

CD 1, Track 48

1. Écoutez bien! p. 66

Isabelle is in a café talking to Jean-Paul. You will hear Isabelle asking questions. For each of Isabelle's questions, select Jean-Paul's response from the suggested answers. She will repeat each question. Écoutez.

1. Quel temps fait-il?
2. Tu veux un sandwich?
3. Tu veux un jus d'orange?
4. Quelle heure est-il?
5. C'est quand, ton anniversaire?
6. Combien coûte le sandwich?

CD 1, Track 49

3. Conversation dirigée, p. 66

Stéphanie is in a café called Le Select. The waiter is taking her order. Écoutez leur conversation.

LE GARÇON: Bonjour, mademoiselle! Vous désirez?
STÉPHANIE: Je voudrais un croissant, s'il vous plaît. Combien coûte un jus d'orange?
LE GARÇON: 2 euros.
STÉPHANIE: Donnez-moi un jus d'orange, s'il vous plaît! . . . Monsieur, s'il vous plaît! Ça fait combien!
LE GARÇON: Ça fait 4 euros cinquante.
STÉPHANIE: Voici 5 euros.
LE GARÇON: Merci, mademoiselle.

Discovering
FRENCH
Nouveau!

BLEU

Unité 2
Leçon 4

Audioscripts

WORKBOOK AUDIO

Vidéo-scène A. L'heure

Section 1. Quelle heure est-il?
(Part 1)

CD 6, Track 16

A. Compréhension orale
Listening Comprehension, **p. 41**

Listen as various people ask others what time it is. Then complete the clock face to indicate the hour that you hear.

Modèle: —Dis, Papa. Quelle heure est-il?
　　　　 —Il est six heures.

You would draw the hour hand pointing to six on the clock.

1. —Dis, Frédéric. Quelle heure est-il?
　 —Il est huit heures. #

2. —Dis, Jean-Claude. Quelle heure est-il? . . . Quelle heure est-il?
　 —Il est une heure. #

3. —Pardon, monsieur. Quelle heure est-il?
　 —Il est midi. #

4. —Pardon, madame. Quelle heure est-il?
　 —Il est onze heures.
　 —Merci. #

5. —Pardon, mademoiselle. Quelle heure est-il?
　 —Il est deux heures.
　 —Merci. #

Now check your answers. You should have filled in the clock faces as follows: 1-8 o'clock, 2-1 o'clock, 3-noon, 4-11 o'clock, and 5-2 o'clock.

CD 6, Track 17

B. Questions et réponses
Questions and answers, **p. 41**

The speaker will ask you what time it is. Answer according to the corresponding picture. Then listen for the confirmation.

Modèle: Quelle heure est-il?
　　　　 (*response*) Il est huit heures.

1. Quelle heure est-il? # Il est dix heures.
2. Quelle heure est-il? # Il est midi.
3. Quelle heure est-il? # Il est une heure.
4. Quelle heure est-il? # Il est trois heures.
5. Quelle heure est-il? # Il est quatre heures.
6. Quelle heure est-il? # Il est neuf heures.
7. Quelle heure est-il? # Il est minuit.

Section 2. Quelle heure est-il?
(Part 2)

CD 6, Track 18

C. Compréhension orale
Listening Comprehension, **p. 41**

Écoutez et répétez. Listen as various people ask others what time it is. Then write in the times on the corresponding digital clocks.

Modèle: —Quelle heure est-il?
　　　　 —Il est une heure et quart.

　 You would write 1:15 in the clock on your worksheet.

1. —Quelle heure est-il?
　 —Il est cinq heures et demie.
　 —Merci. #

2. —Quelle heure est-il?
　 —Il est sept heures moins le quart. #

Discovering
FRENCH
Nouveau!

BLEU

3. —Pardon, monsieur. Quelle heure est-il?
   —Il est quatre heures cinq. #

4. —Quelle heure est-il?
   —Il est trois heures cinquante. #

Now check your answers. You should have written in the following times: 1-5:30, 2-6:45, 3-4:05, 4-3:50.

CD 6, Track 19

D. Questions et réponses
Questions and answers, **p. 42**

The speaker will ask you what time it is. Answer according to the corresponding picture. Then listen for the confirmation.

Modèle: Quelle heure est-il?
(*response*) Il est huit heures et quart.

1. Quelle heure est-il? # Il est dix heures et quart.
2. Quelle heure est-il? # Il est onze heures et demie.
3. Quelle heure est-il? # Il est deux heures moins le quart.
4. Quelle heure est-il? # Il est six heures dix.
5. Quelle heure est-il? # Il est neuf heures vingt.
6. Quelle heure est-il? # Il est dix heures quarante.

Section 3. À quelle heure?

CD 6, Track 20

E. Compréhension orale
Listening Comprehension, **p. 42**

Listen to the dialogues to find out when the following events are going to take place. Then write the times in the spaces provided.

Modèle: STÉPHANIE: Et à quelle heure est le film?
DAVID: À quatre heures et quart.

1. —Dis, Marc, à quelle heure est la classe de français?
   —À onze heures. #

2. —Dis, Maman, à quelle heure est le dîner?
   —À sept heures et demie. #

3. —Dis, Anne, à quelle heure est le film?
   —À neuf heures dix. #

4. —Pardon, madame, à quelle heure est le train de Toulouse?
   —À six heures moins le quart.
   —Merci. #

Now check your answers. You should have written: 1-11:00, 2-7:30, 3-9:10, and 4-5:45.

Section 4. Dictée

CD 6, Track 21

F. Écoutez et écrivez.
Listen and write. **p. 42**

You will hear a short dialogue spoken twice. First listen carefully to what the people are saying. The second time you hear the dialogue, fill in the missing words.

Écoutez.
   —Dis, Philippe, quelle heure est-il?
   —Il est cinq heures moins le quart.
   —Et à quelle heure est le film?
   —À sept heures et demie.
   —Merci!

Listen again and fill in the missing words.

Vidéo-scène B. Le jour et la date

Section 1. Les jours de la semaine

CD 6, Track 22

A. Compréhension orale
Listening comprehension, **p. 45**

Philippe has many cousins and they are all arriving this week. Listen carefully and then draw a line connecting each name to the appropriate day of the week. Here is a model.

Modèle: Christine arrive mardi.

You would draw a line from Christine to mardi.

1. Pauline arrive jeudi. #
2. Bertrand arrive mercredi. #
3. Céline arrive dimanche. #
4. Didier arrive lundi. #
5. Agnès arrive mardi. #
6. Guillaume arrive samedi. #
7. Véronique arrive vendredi. #

Now check your answers. You should have connected the names as follows: 1-d, 2-c, 3-g, 4-a, 5-b, 6-f, and 7-e.

Section 2. La date

CD 6, Track 23

B. Compréhension orale
Listening comprehension, **p. 45**

In the following dialogues, people are giving the date. Listen carefully and complete the sentences in your Workbook according to what you hear.

Modèle: Quel jour est-ce aujourd'hui?
C'est le deux février.
You would write the number "2."

1. C'est le 22 mars. #

2. C'est le trois juin. #

3. C'est le premier juillet. #

4. C'est le sept août.
—Mais non, c'est le huit août.
—Ah oui, c'est vrai. C'est le huit août. #

5. C'est le trois septembre.
—C'est vrai. C'est le trois septembre. #

6. C'est le quatre novembre. #

Now check your answers. 1-March 22, 2-June 3, 3-July 1, 4-August 8, 5-September 3, 6-November 4.

CD 6, Track 24

C. Questions et réponses
Questions and answers, **p. 46**

Now it's your turn to give the dates. Look at the calendar pages in your Workbook and respond accordingly. Then listen for the confirmation.

Modèle: Quel jour est-ce?
(*response*) C'est le 5 décembre.

1. Quel jour est-ce? # C'est le 26 avril.
2. Quel jour est-ce? # C'est le 16 août.
3. Quel jour est-ce? # C'est le 14 mai.
4. Quel jour est-ce? # C'est le 21 juillet.
5. Quel jour est-ce? # C'est le 12 septembre.
6. Quel jour est-ce? # C'est le premier octobre.
7. Quel jour est-ce? # C'est le 30 janvier.

Section 3. L'anniversaire

CD 6, Track 25

D. Compréhension orale
Listening Comprehension, **p. 46**

Listen as the following people tell you their birthdays. Write down each date in the space provided. Use French abbreviations.

Listen to the model.

Modèle: —Alice, c'est quand ton anniversaire?
—C'est le 18 juillet.

You would write eighteen-slash-seven in the blank.

Commençons. (*Let's begin.*)

1. —Béatrice, c'est quand ton anniversaire?
—C'est le 23 décembre. #
2. —Françoise, c'est quand ton anniversaire?
—C'est le premier mars. #

Unité 2
Leçon 4

Audioscripts

Discovering
FRENCH
Nouveau!

B L E U

3. —Julie, c'est quand ton anniversaire?
   —C'est le 13 mai. #
4. —Delphine, c'est quand ton
   anniversaire?
   —C'est le 29 juin. #
5. —Denis, c'est quand ton anniversaire?
   —C'est le 6 novembre. #
6. —Paul, c'est quand ton anniversaire?
   —C'est le 15 août. #

Now check your answers. You should have
written:

Béatrice: 23-slash-12, December 23rd;
Françoise: 1-slash-3, March 1st;
Julie: 13-slash-5, May 13th;
Delphine: 29-slash-6, June 29th;
Denis: 6-slash-11, November 6th;
Paul: 15-slash-8, August 15th.

Section 4. Conversations

CD 6, Track 26

E. Compréhension orale
Listening Comprehension, **p. 47**

You will hear a conversation between David
and Charlotte. Listen to each section of the
conversation carefully. Then answer the
corresponding questions in your Workbook
by circling the appropriate letter (a, b or c).
You will hear each section of the
conversation twice.

Commençons. (*Let's begin.*)

1. —Quel jour est-ce aujourd'hui?
   —C'est vendredi.

Listen again.

2. —Dis, Charlotte, c'est quand, ton
   anniversaire?
   —C'est le 5 octobre.

Listen again.

3. —Et toi, David, c'est quand, ton
   anniversaire?
   —C'est le premier août.

Listen again.

4. —Au revoir, David.
   —Au revoir, Charlotte. À demain!
   —À demain.

Listen again.

Now check your answers. You should have
circled 1-c, 2-b, 3-b, and 4-a.

Section 5. Dictée

CD 6, Track 27

F. Écoutez et écrivez.
Listen and write. **p. 47**

You will hear a short dialogue spoken twice.
First listen carefully to what the people are
saying. The second time you hear the
dialogue, fill in the missing words.

Écoutez.

—C'est quand, ton anniversaire?

—C'est le deux juin. C'est un dimanche.
Et toi?

—Moi, c'est le premier novembre. C'est un
vendredi.

Listen again and fill in the missing words.

Vidéo-scène C. Le temps

Section 1. Quel temps fait-il?

CD 6, Track 28

A. Compréhension orale
Listening Comprehension, **p. 51**

Now listen as various people talk about the
weather. Draw a line connecting the date to
the corresponding weather condition.

Modèle: —C'est le premier avril.
—Quel temps fait-il?
—Il pleut.

You would draw a line from April 1 to "f": the picture of rain.

1. —C'est le 24 novembre.
—Quel temps fait-il?
—Il fait mauvais. #

2. —C'est le 15 septembre aujourd'hui.
—Quel temps fait-il?
—Il fait beau. #

3. —C'est le 13 juin.
—Quel temps fait-il aujourd'hui?
—Il fait bon. #

4. —C'est le 20 juillet.
—Quel temps fait-il aujourd'hui?
—Il fait chaud. #

5. —C'est le 8 mars. Il fait frais aujourd'hui. #

6. —C'est le 17 décembre.
—Quel temps fait-il?
—Il fait froid. #

7. —C'est le 2 octobre.
—Quel temps fait-il?
—Il pleut. #

8. —C'est le 12 janvier.
—Quel temps fait-il?
—Il neige. #

Now check your answers. You should have connected November 24 to g; September 15 to d; June 13 to b; July 20 to c; March 8 to a; December 17 to h; October 2 to f; and January 12 to e.

CD 6, Track 29

B. Questions et réponses
Questions and answers, **p. 52**

Now it's your turn to talk about the weather. Look at the illustrations in your Workbook and describe the weather. Then listen for the confirmation.

1. Quel temps fait-il? # Il fait chaud.
2. Quel temps fait-il? # Il fait froid.

3. Quel temps fait-il? # Il fait beau.
4. Quel temps fait-il? # Il fait mauvais.
5. Quel temps fait-il? # Il pleut.
6. Quel temps fait-il? # Il neige.

Section 2. Conversations

CD 6, Track 30

C. Compréhension orale
Listening Comprehension, **p. 52**

You will hear a series of short conversations between Jean-Paul and Céline. Listen to each conversation carefully. Then answer the corresponding questions in your Workbook by circling the appropriate letter (a, b or c). You will hear each conversation twice.

Commençons. (*Let's begin.*)

1. —Quelle heure est-il?
—Il est trois heures et quart.

Listen again.

2. —Quel temps fait-il?
—Il fait froid.

Listen again.

3. —Quel temps fait-il à Paris?
—Il pleut.

Listen again.

4. —Quelle est ta saison préférée?
—C'est l'automne.

Listen again.

Now check your answers. You should have circled 1-c, 2-b, 3-a and 4-c.

Section 3. Dictée

CD 6, Track 31

D. Écoutez et écrivez.
Listen and write. **p. 52**

You will hear a short dialogue spoken twice. First listen carefully to what the people are saying. The second time you hear the dialogue, fill in the missing words.

Écoutez.
—Quel temps fait-il aujourd'hui?
—Il fait beau.
—Et en automne?
—Il pleut.

Listen again and fill in the missing words.

(Repeat the dialogue, pausing after each exchange.)

LESSON 4 QUIZ

Part I: Listening

CD 13, Track 13

A. L'heure

You will hear a series of short conversations where people are talking about the time. Listen carefully, and indicate the time on the corresponding clock face. You will hear each conversation twice.

Let's begin:

1. —Quelle heure est-il?
   —Il est quatre heures.

2. —Quelle heure est-il?
   —Il est cinq heures moins le quart.

3. —Quelle heure est-il, Stéphanie?
   —Il est midi.

4. —À quelle heure est le match de tennis?
   —À deux heures et demie.

5. —À quelle heure est le film?
   —À huit heures vingt.

CD 13, Track 14

B. Conversations

You will hear a series of short conversations between Éric and Valérie. Listen to each conversation carefully. Then answer the corresponding questions on your answer sheet by circling the appropriate letter (a, b, or c). You will hear each conversation twice.

Let's begin.

1. VALÉRIE: Quel jour est-ce aujourd'hui?
   ÉRIC: C'est mercredi.

2. ÉRIC: Dis, Valérie, c'est quand, ton anniversaire?
   VALÉRIE: C'est le 5 juillet.

3. VALÉRIE: Tu as rendez-vous avec Marc aujourd'hui?
   ÉRIC: Non, j'ai rendez-vous dimanche.

4. VALÉRIE: Oh là là, il fait chaud aujourd'hui!
   ÉRIC: Oui, j'ai soif. Donne-moi un soda, s'il te plaît.

5. ÉRIC: Il fait mauvais?
   VALÉRIE: Oui, il pleut!

Nom _____

Classe _____   Date _____

QUIZ 4

Part I: Listening

A. L'heure (25 points)

You will hear a series of short conversations where people are talking about the time. Listen carefully, and indicate the time on the corresponding clock face. You will hear each conversation twice.

1.
2.
3.
4.
5.

B. Conversations (25 points)

You will hear a series of short conversations between Éric and Valérie. Listen to each conversation carefully. Then answer the corresponding questions on your answer sheet by circling the appropriate letter (a, b, or c). You will hear each conversation twice.

1. What day is today?
   a. Tuesday
   b. Wednesday
   c. Saturday

2. When is Valérie's birthday?
   a. January 5
   b. June 15
   c. July 5

3. When is Éric meeting Marc?
   a. today
   b. Saturday
   c. Sunday

4. How is the weather today?
   a. It's hot.
   b. It's so-so.
   c. It's windy.

5. According to the weather, what should people wear today?
   a. light clothes
   b. a winter jacket
   c. a raincoat

Nom _____

Classe _____ Date _____

Part II: Writing

C. Le temps (30 points)

Describe the weather in each picture.

1. _____

2. _____

3. _____

4. _____

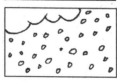

5. _____

D. Expression personnelle (20 points)

Answer the following questions in French. Use complete sentences.

• Quel jour est-ce aujourd'hui?

_____

• C'est quand, ton anniversaire?

_____

UNITÉ 2
La vie courante

CULTURAL CONTEXT: Having a snack in France

FUNCTIONS:

- saying you are hungry or thirsty
- asking for something to eat or drink
- ordering in a café and paying the check
- telling time
- talking about dates, birthdays, days of the week
- talking about the weather

RELATED THEMES:

- common foods
- common beverages
- days of the week
- months of the year
- seasons and weather expressions

 **POUR COMMUNIQUER** **Communicative Expressions and Thematic Vocabulary**

Nom _____

Classe _____ Date _____

Discovering
FRENCH
Nouveau!

B L E U

UNITÉ 2 Interviews

In this section you will be interviewed by different
people who want to get to know you better. If you
wish, you may write the answers to the interview
questions in the space provided.

Interview 1

We are in a French restaurant and I would like to
treat you. Let me know what you would like to eat and drink.

- **Tu veux un sandwich ou un hamburger?**
- **Tu veux une omelette ou une salade?**
- **Tu veux une limonade ou un soda?**
- **Tu veux un jus d'orange ou un jus de pomme?**

AU RESTAURANT

• _____

• _____

• _____

• _____

À LA CAMPAGNE
Restaurant végétarien

AU PALAIS DES GLACES
spécialités de glaces

À la Normandie
spécialités de fromages

Au petit gourmand
ses glaces et ses gâteaux

Discovering
FRENCH
Nouveau!

B L E U

Unité 2
Resources

Communipak

Interview 2

I am a French classmate of yours and I run into you in the hall. I am in a hurry because I think I am late for our class. Answer my greeting and my questions.

- **Salut [name of partner]! Ça va?**
- **Quelle heure est-il?**
- **À quelle heure est la classe?**

- Ça va? _____

- L'heure:

- L'heure de la classe:

PONT DE
L'ARCHEVECHE

QUELLE
HEURE
EST-IL

LYCÉE JEAN-BAPTISTE COROT

Étudiante: AUBIN, Nathalie

	LUNDI	MARDI	MERCREDI	JEUDI	VENDREDI	SAMEDI
8h30 à 9h30	Histoire	Allemand		Informatique*		Français
9h30 à 10h30	Anglais	Français	Anglais	Physique	Allemand	Français
10h30 à 11h30	Sport	Français	informatique	Maths	Latin	Latin
11h30 à 12h30	Français	Latin	Maths		Sciences vie et terre	Histoire ou civilisation
13h00 à 14h00						
14h00 à 15h00	Sciences vie et terre	Maths		Allemand		
15h00 à 16h00	Géographie	Maths				
16h00 à 17h00	Physique	Anglais		Sport		

Nom _____

Classe _____ Date _____

Interview 3

I do not have a pocket calendar and I have trouble keeping track of dates. Can you answer my questions?

- **Quel jour est-ce aujourd'hui?**
- **Quelle est la date?**
- **C'est quand, ton anniversaire?**

- Aujourd'hui: _____

- Date: _____

- Date d'anniversaire: _____

Interview 4

I also have trouble keeping track of dates. Can you answer my questions?

- **Quel jour est-ce demain?**
- **Quelle est la date demain?**
- **C'est quand, ton anniversaire?**

- Demain: _____

- Date: _____

- Date d'anniversaire: _____

Nom _____

Classe _____ Date _____

Discovering
FRENCH *Nouveau!*

B L E U

Unité 2
Resources

Communipak

Interview 5

I am new in this region and do not know much
about the weather.

- **Quel temps fait-il aujourd'hui?**
- **Quel temps fait-il en hiver?**
- **Quel temps fait-il en été?**
- **Quel temps fait-il en automne?**

LE TEMPS

- Aujourd'hui: _____

- En hiver: _____

- En été: _____

- En automne: _____

LA MÉTÉO
au Québec

dimanche

PLUIE

Nom _____

Classe _____ Date _____

Discovering
FRENCH
Nouveau!

B L E U

Tu as la parole

Read the instructions on the cards below, and give your partner the corresponding information in French. Take turns reading your cards and listening to each other.

| **TU AS LA PAROLE 1** | **UNITÉ 2** |

It is August and you are at the local swimming pool with a French friend.

- Say that it is hot.
- Mention that you are thirsty.
- Say that you would like a soda.

| **TU AS LA PAROLE 2** | **UNITÉ 2** |

It is noon. You are walking downtown with your French friend and come to a hamburger stand.

- Say that it is noon and that you are hungry.
- Say that you would like a hamburger.
- Ask your friend to lend you 3 euros.

| **TU AS LA PAROLE 3** | **UNITÉ 2** |

You are in a French café.

- Order a dish of your choice.
- Order a beverage of your choice.
- Ask how much it costs.

| **TU AS LA PAROLE 4** | **UNITÉ 2** |

You are reading the menu in a French café. Name . . .

- two meat dishes
- two other dishes
- two beverages

Nom _____

Classe _____ Date _____

Discovering
FRENCH
Nouveau!

BLEU

Unité 2
Resources

Communipak

TU AS LA PAROLE 5   UNITÉ 2

Name your favorite day, month, and season.

- **Mon jour préféré est le . . .**
- **Mon mois préféré est le (l') . . .**
- **Ma saison préférée est le (l') . . .**

TU AS LA PAROLE 6   UNITÉ 2

Select three seasons of the year. For each season, describe the weather in a region of your choice.

-
-
-

TU AS LA PAROLE 7   UNITÉ 2

Let's talk about today.

- What day of the week is it today?
- What time is it now?
- How is the weather?

TU AS LA PAROLE 8   UNITÉ 2

Give the birthdays of the following people.

- **Mon anniversaire, c'est . . .**
- **L'anniversaire de mon copain, c'est . . .**
- **L'anniversaire de ma copine, c'est . . .**

Nom _____

Classe _____ Date _____

Conversations

Act out the following situations with your partner. Take turns:

- In the odd-numbered situations, you will be asking the questions.
- In the even-numbered situations, you will be answering your partner's questions.

CONVERSATION 1   UNITÉ 2

You have invited a French exchange student to a picnic.

◆ ━━━━━━━━━━━━━━━━━━━━━━━━━━━━━━━━━━ ◆

Ask your partner . . .

- if he/she is thirsty
- if he/she is hungry
- if he/she wants a sandwich
- if he/she wants a soda

CONVERSATION 2

You are a student from Quebec and your friend has invited you to have dinner at his/her home.

Answer your partner's questions.

CONVERSATION 3   UNITÉ 2

You are in a French restaurant with your French friend,
who is reading the menu.

◆ ━━━━━━━━━━━━━━━━━━━━━━━━━━━━━━━━━━ ◆

Ask your partner . . .

- how much the steak and French fries cost
- how much the salad costs

Then ask your partner . . .

- to loan you 10 euros

CONVERSATION 4

You have just been introduced to a French tourist who is visiting your city. Answer your partner's questions.

Unité 2 Resources
Communipak

Discovering French, Nouveau! Bleu

Nom _____

Classe _____ Date _____

Discovering FRENCH *Nouveau!*

B L E U

Side A

Unité 2 Resources Communipak

CONVERSATION 5 **UNITÉ 2**

Your friend is phoning to invite you to dinner and to a concert afterwards.

◆━━━━━━━━━━━━━━━◆

Ask your partner . . .

- what time it is
- at what time the dinner **(le dîner)** is
- at what time the concert **(le concert)** is

CONVERSATION 6

You and your friend are planning to go to the movies. Right now you are sitting in a café.

Answer your partner's questions.

CONVERSATION 7 **UNITÉ 2**

You are spending the month of August at a summer camp in Quebec. Today you are waking up late.

Ask your partner . . .

◆━━━━━━━━━━━━━━━◆

- what time it is
- what day it is
- how the weather is

CONVERSATION 8

Your friend is phoning to invite you to his/her birthday party.

Answer your partner's questions.

Nom _____

Classe _____ Date _____

Discovering
FRENCH
Nouveau!

B L E U

Side B

Conversations

Act out the following situations with your partner. Take turns:

- In the odd-numbered situations, you will be answering your partner's questions.
- In the even-numbered situations, you will be asking the questions.

CONVERSATION 1

You are a French student visiting the United States. Your friend has invited you to a picnic.

Answer your partner's questions affirmatively.

CONVERSATION 2   UNITÉ 2

You have invited a friend from Quebec to have dinner at your home.

◆────────────────────────────◆

Ask your partner . . .

- if he/she wants a steak or a pizza
- if he/she wants a crepe or an ice cream
- if he/she wants (a glass of) orange juice or (a glass of) apple juice

---

CONVERSATION 3

You are a French student. You are in a restaurant with your American friend and are looking at the menu.

Answer your partner's questions (inventing prices, as appropriate).

CONVERSATION 4   UNITÉ 2

You are a French tourist visiting this city.

◆────────────────────────────◆

Ask your partner (who lives here) . . .

- how the weather is in winter
- how the weather is in fall
- how the weather is in summer

Nom _____

Classe _____ Date _____

Discovering
FRENCH *Nouveau!*

BLEU

Side B

Unité 2
Resources

Communipak

CONVERSATION 5

Your friend is phoning to invite you to dinner and to a concert afterwards.

Answer your partner's questions.

CONVERSATION 6   UNITÉ 2

You and your friend are planning to go to the movies.
Right now you are sitting in a café.

◆————————————————————————◆

Ask your partner . . .

- what time it is
- at what time the movie **(le film)** is
- how much the ticket **(le billet)** costs

CONVERSATION 7

You are spending the month of August at a summer camp in Quebec. Today you are waking up late.

Answer your partner's questions.

CONVERSATION 8   UNITÉ 2

Your friend is phoning to invite you to his/her birthday
party.

◆————————————————————————◆

Ask your partner . . .

- when his/her birthday is
- what day (of the week) the party **(le dîner)** is
- at what time

Nom _____

Classe _____ Date _____

Échanges

1 Imagine you are at a French café with five of your friends. You are in charge of taking the order.

> • Ask your friends what they each would like to eat.
>
> • Ask them what they each would like to drink.
>
> • Record the orders on the chart below.

NOM		
▶ Bob	une glace	un jus d'orange
1		
2		
3		
4		
5		

Nom _____

Classe _____ Date _____

Discovering
FRENCH
Nouveau!

B L E U

Unité 2
Resources

Communipak

2 Imagine you are a French journalist. You are writing an article about American meal times.

- Select four classmates and ask them when they have dinner.
- Record their answers on the clocks in the chart below.

> À quelle heure dînes-tu?

> Je dîne à six heures et demie.

NOM	HEURE DU DÎNER
1	
2	
3	
4	

Nom _____

Classe _____ Date _____

3 You want to know when different friends' birthdays are.

- Ask five friends when their birthdays are.
- Record their answers on the information sheet below.

ANNIVERSAIRES	
NOM	**DATE D'ANNIVERSAIRE**
▶ Patricia Jackson	le 18 octobre
1	
2	
3	
4	
5	

Nom _____

Classe _____ Date _____

Discovering
FRENCH
Nouveau!

B L E U

Unité 2
Resources

Communipak

4 The weather often influences what we like to drink.

- Have three classmates tell you what beverage they would like under the various weather conditions illustrated in the chart.
- Record their answers on the chart.

Il fait chaud.
Je voudrais une limonade.

	NOMS		
	1.	**2.**	**3.**

Nom _____

Classe _____ Date _____

Tête à tête

1 **Combien coûte . . . ?**

a

You are in a French café. Your partner has the menu.

■ Select three beverages and ask your partner how much each one costs.

> **Combien coûte le jus d'orange?**

 Write the prices on the appropriate lines.

b

You are in a French restaurant. Your partner will ask you how much three of the following items cost.

■ Give your partner the prices.

MENU

 3 euros

 4,50 euros

 5,20 euros

 2,60 euros

 2,75 euros

Nom _____

Classe _____ Date _____

Discovering FRENCH Nouveau!

BLEU

Élève B

Unité 2 Resources Communipak

Tête à tête

1 Combien coûte . . . ?

a

You are in a French café. Your partner will ask you how much three of the following items cost.

■ Give your partner the prices.

b

You are in a French restaurant. Your partner has the menu.

■ Select three items and ask your partner how much each one costs.

Combien coûte un hamburger?

Write the prices on the appropriate lines.

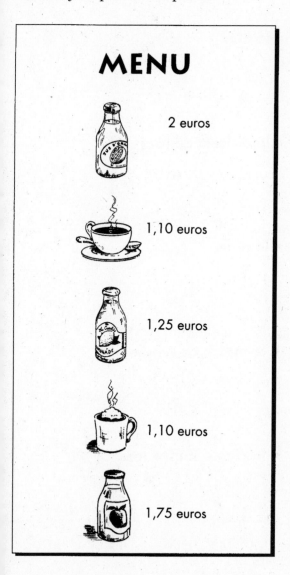

MENU

2 euros

1,10 euros

1,25 euros

1,10 euros

1,75 euros

Tête à tête

2 **À quelle heure?**

■ Ask your partner when the following events are taking place.

À quelle heure est le pique-nique?

 Fill in the clocks accordingly.

• **le pique-nique**

• **le match de volley**

• **la classe de maths**

• **le concert de rock**

• **le récital**

You know when the following events are taking place, but your partner does not.

■ Your partner will ask what time each event is. Answer the questions.

• **le film**

• **le concert de jazz**

• **le dîner**

• **le match de tennis**

• **la classe de français**

Nom _____

Classe _____ Date _____

Discovering FRENCH *Nouveau!*

B L E U

Élève B

Tête à tête

 2 **À quelle heure?**

a

You know when the following events are taking place, but your partner does not.

■ Your partner will ask what time each event is. Answer the questions.

- **le pique-nique**

- **le match de volley**

- **la classe de maths**

- **le concert de rock**

- **le récital**

b

■ Ask your partner when the following events are taking place.

À quelle heure est le film?

 Fill in the clocks accordingly.

- **le film**

- **le concert de jazz**

- **le dîner**

- **le match de tennis**

- **la classe de français**

Nom _____

Classe _____ Date _____

Discovering
FRENCH *Nouveau!*

BLEU

Élève A

Tête à tête

3 Joyeux anniversaire!

You and your partner are going to
talk about birthdays.

 First complete the sentences
below with the appropriate dates.
(If you are not sure, invent an answer!)

• **Mon anniversaire est** _____

• **L'anniversaire de mon copain est** _____

• **L'anniversaire de ma mère est** _____

■ Now answer your partner's questions

b

■ Now it's your turn to ask your partner about some birthdays.

> **C'est quand, ton anniversaire?**

 Record the information your partner gives you in the appropriate boxes.

• **ton anniversaire?** _____

• **l'anniversaire de ton cousin?** _____

• **l'anniversaire de ta copine?** _____

Nom _____

Classe _____ Date _____

Discovering
FRENCH
Nouveau!

BLEU

Unité 2
Resources

Communipak

Tête à tête

3 Joyeux anniversaire!

Élève B

a

You and your partner are going to talk about birthdays.

■ First, you will ask your partner about certain birthdays.

C'est quand, ton anniversaire?

Record the information your partner gives you in the appropriate boxes.

• **ton anniversaire?** _____

• **l'anniversaire de ton copain?** _____

• **l'anniversaire de ta mère?** _____

b

Now your partner is going to ask you about some people's birthdays.

First complete the sentences below with the appropriate dates. (If you are not sure, invent an answer!)

• **Mon anniversaire est** _____

• **L'anniversaire de mon cousin est** _____

• **L'anniversaire de ma copine est** _____

■ Now answer your partner's questions.

Nom _____

Classe _____ Date _____

Tête à tête

4 ▊ Quel temps fait-il?

a

You would like to know what the weather is like in certain French cities.

■ Ask your partner, who lives there.

> **Quel temps fait-il à Nice?**

 Write down the information your partner gives you.

- à Nice? _____
- à Lille? _____
- à Deauville? _____
- à Albertville? _____
- à Bordeaux? _____

b

You are a student living in Canada. Your partner will ask you how the weather is in different cities.

■ Consult the following weather map as you answer your partner's questions. (You may want to write out your responses next to the names of the cities.)

- À Québec _____
- À Vancouver _____
- À Toronto _____
- À Calgary _____
- À Montréal _____

Nom

Classe _____ Date _____

Discovering FRENCH *Nouveau!*

BLEU

Unité 2
Resources
Communipak

Tête à tête

Élève B

4 | Quel temps fait-il?

a

You are a student living in France. Your partner will ask you how the weather is in different cities.

■ Consult the following weather map as you answer your partner's questions. (You may want to write out your responses next to the names of the cities.)

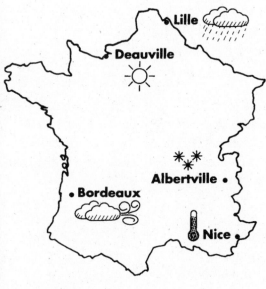

- À Nice _____

- À Lille _____

- À Deauville _____

- À Albertville _____

- À Bordeaux _____

b

You would like to know what the weather is like in certain Canadian cities.

■ Ask your partner, who lives there.

Quel temps fait-il à Québec?

Write down the information your partner give you.

- à Québec? _____

- à Vancouver? _____

- à Toronto? _____

- à Calgary _____

- à Montréal? _____

URB
p. 153

Discovering FRENCH
Nouveau!

BLEU

Nom _____

Classe _____ Date _____

Communicative Expressions and Thematic Vocabulary

Saying that you are hungry and thirsty

Tu as faim?	*Are you hungry?*	J'ai faim.	*I'm hungry.*
Tu as soif?	*Are you thirsty?*	J'ai soif.	*I'm thirsty.*

Offering a friend something to eat or drink

Qu'est-ce que tu veux?	*What do you want?*
Tu veux [une pizza]?	*Do you want [a pizza]?*

Asking a friend for something

Je voudrais [une salade].	*I would like [a salad].*
S'il te plaît, donne-moi [un sandwich].	*Please, give me [a sandwich].*
Prête-moi [5 euros], s'il te plaît.	*Please, lend (loan) me [5 euros].*

Ordering in a café

Vous désirez?	*May I help you?*
Je voudrais [un jus d'orange].	*I would like [an orange juice].*
S'il vous plaît, donnez-moi [un café].	*Please, give me [a coffee].*

Asking how much something costs

C'est combien?	*How much is it?*
Ça fait combien?	*How much does that come to (make)?*
Ça fait [3 euros].	*That's [3 euros]. That comes to [3 euros].*
Combien coûte [le thé / la limonade]?	*How much does [the tea / the lemon soda] cost?*
Il / Elle coûte [un euro].	*It costs [1 euro].*

Les nourritures

un croissant	*croissant [crescent roll]*	une crêpe	*crêpe [thin pancake]*
un hamburger	*hamburger*	une glace	*ice cream*
un hot dog	*hot dog*	une omelette	*omelet*
un sandwich	*sandwich*	une pizza	*pizza*
un steak	*steak*	une salade	*salad*
un steak-frites	*steak and fries*		

Les boissons

un café	*coffee*	un jus d'orange	*orange juice*	une limonade	*lemon soda*
un chocolat	*hot chocolate*	un jus de pomme	*apple juice*		
un soda	*soft drink*	un jus de raisin	*grape juice*		
un thé	*tea*	un jus de tomate	*tomato juice*		

Nom _____

Classe _____ Date _____

Discovering FRENCH *Nouveau!*

BLEU

Unité 2
Resources

Communipak

Talking about the time

Quelle heure est-il?		What time is it?	
Il est	une heure.	It's	one o'clock.
	huit heures du matin.		eight (o'clock) in the morning.
	deux heures de l'après-midi.		two (o'clock) in the afternoon.
	dix heures du soir.		ten (o'clock) in the evening.
	trois heures et quart.		quarter past three.
	cinq heures et demie.		half past five.
	sept heures moins le quart.		quarter of seven.
	midi.		noon.
	minuit.		midnight.

À quelle heure est [le film]? — *At what time is [the movie]?*
J'ai un rendez-vous à neuf heures. — *I have an appointment (a date) at nine.*

Talking about days of the week

Quel jour est-ce?		What day is it?	
Aujourd'hui, c'est	lundi.	Today is	Monday.
Demain, c'est	mardi.	Tomorrow is	Tuesday.
	mercredi.		Wednesday.
	jeudi.		Thursday.
	vendredi.		Friday.
	samedi.		Saturday.
	dimanche.		Sunday.

Telling people when you will see them again

À samedi!   *See you Saturday!*   À demain!   *See you tomorrow!*

Talking about birthdays

C'est quand, ton anniversaire? — *When's your birthday?*
Mon anniversaire est le [5 août]. — *My birthday is [August 5].*

Talking about the weather

Quel temps fait-il? *How's the weather?*

Il fait beau.	It's beautiful out.	Il fait frais.	It's cool.	Il pleut.	It's raining.
Il fait bon.	It's warm.	Il fait froid.	It's cold.	Il neige.	It's snowing.
Il fait chaud.	It's hot.	Il fait mauvais.	It's terrible out.		

Les saisons

le printemps	spring	au printemps	in (the) spring
l'été	summer	en été	in (the) summer
l'automne	fall, autumn	en automne	in (the) fall
l'hiver	winter	en hiver	in (the) winter

Nom _____

Classe _____ Date _____

Discovering
FRENCH
Nouveau!

BLEU

VOCABULAIRE SUPPLÉMENTAIRE: *Les parties du corps*

le bras	*arm*	le nez	*nose*	la bouche	*mouth*
les cheveux	*hair*	un oeil (les yeux)	*eye(s)*	la jambe	*leg*
le cou	*neck*	le pied	*foot*	la main	*hand*
le dos	*back*	le ventre	*stomach*	une oreille	*ear*
				la tête	*head*

Talking about the date

Quelle est la date?		*What's the date?*		
C'est le premier	janvier.	*It's the first of*	*January.*	*(January first)*
C'est le deux	février.	*It's the second of*	*February.*	*(February second)*
	mars		*March*	
	avril		*April*	
	mai		*May*	
	juin		*June*	
	juillet		*July*	
	août		*August*	
	septembre		*September*	
	octobre		*October*	
	novembre		*November*	
	décembre		*December*	

Nom _____

Classe _____ Date _____

Discovering
FRENCH *Nouveau!*

B L E U

Unité 2
Resources

Activités pour tous TE
Reading

UNITÉ 2   Reading Comprehension

A

A. *Restaurant* **LA TOUR DE JADE**
Cuisine vietnamienne et chinoise de grande classe
Plat à emporter   碧玉臺   fermé le dimanche midi
20, rue de la Michodière - 75002 PARIS
Métro : Opéra ou Quatre Septembre   **01 47 42 07 56**

B. *Le Flore en l'Ile*
SALON DE THE   Glaces & Sorbets de la maison
RESTAURANT
GLACIER   **Berthillon°**
42, quai d'Orléans   ouvert tous les jours de 8h à 2h
Ile Saint-Louis   **01 43 29 88 27**
75004 PARIS   Fax : 01 43 29 73 54

C. *Piccolo Teatro*
Restaurant végétarien
6, rue des Ecouffes - 75004 PARIS
01 42 72 17 79
Ouvert 12h-15h - 19h-23h30
Fermé lundi

Compréhension

1. Which of the three restaurants caters to Asian tastes?
   La Tour de Jade

2. If you don't eat meat, which restaurant would you prefer?
   Piccolo Teatro

3. Which restaurant is open every day?
   Le Flore en l'Île

4. Between the two restaurants that list their hours, which opens earlier?
   Le Flore en l'Île (8h)

5. Which stays open later?
   Piccolo Teatro (23h30)

Qu'est-ce que vous en pensez?

1. What do you think **plat à emporter** means?
   (take-out food)   imported food

2. What do you think **de la maison** means?
   homemade food   (house special)

3. Judging by the postal codes, which two restaurants are probably closest to each other?
   A and B   (B and C)   A and C

Nom _____

Classe _____ Date _____ _____

Discovering
FRENCH
Nouveau!

BLEU

B

Compréhension

1. In 12-hour clock time, what time is it?
   Il est trois heures vingt et un.   (Il est cinq heures vingt et un.)

2. What time of day is it?
   le matin   (l'après-midi)

3. You would consult this board if you were:
   (meeting someone)   seeing someone off

4. Why isn't the arrival gate posted for the Amsterdam train?
   Because it was cancelled.   (Because it is late.)

5. What are the station stops for the train coming from Brussels?
   Mons, Aulnoye et St-Quentin

Qu'est-ce que vous en pensez?

1. Do the trains seems to run, for the most part, on time or with delays? _on time_

2. Circle three other countries besides France that use this station.
   (England)   (Belgium)   Italy
   Germany   (Netherlands)   Spain

3. When talking about transportation, how would you say "origin" and "destination" in French?
   provenance, destination

URB
p. 158

30   Unité 2 Resources
      Activités pour tous Reading   Discovering French, Nouveau! Bleu

Nom _____

Classe _____ Date _____

Discovering FRENCH *Nouveau!*

BLEU

Unité 2 Resources

Activités pour tous TE

Reading

C

Compréhension

1. What day is it? *jeudi*

2. What month is it? *février*

3. Are the temperatures in °F or °C? *°C*

4. How cold is the weather in Montreal, in °F [°F = (°C x 1.8) + 32]? *6.8°F*

5. How cold is the weather in Vancouver, in °F [°F = (°C x 1.8) + 32]? *37.4°F*

Qu'est-ce que vous en pensez?

1. What do you think **venteux** means in Canadian French?

   stormy   (windy)   foggy

2. What do you think **brouillard** means in French?

   (fog)   wind   rain

3. What do you think **pluie** means in French?

   fog   wind   (rain)

URB
p. 159

Nom _____

Classe _____ Date _____

Discovering
FRENCH *Nouveau!*

B L E U

Unité 2
Resources

Workbook TE
Reading and Culture Activities

UNITÉ 2 Reading and Culture Activities

A. À la Terrasse Mailloux

The Terrasse Mailloux is a restaurant in Quebec City. This morning you visited the Citadelle with a classmate, and now you have stopped at the Terrasse Mailloux for lunch.

Together with your classmate, read the menu carefully and select three dishes that you will each have.

- Write down the dishes you have selected.
- Then enter the prices in Canadian dollars for what you have chosen and total up each bill.

MOI		MON COPAIN/MA COPINE	
PLAT	**PRIX**	**PLAT**	**PRIX**
Answers will vary.		Answers will vary.	
TOTAL		**TOTAL**	

Terrasse Mailloux

entrées

Frites (French fries)	0.80
Frites avec sauce hot chicken (French fries with hot chicken sauce)	1.00
Frites avec sauce spaghetti (French fries with spaghetti sauce)	1.65
Oignons français (Onion rings)	1.50

salades

Au poulet (Chicken)	3.95
Au homard (en saison) Lobster (in season)	9.50
Salade du chef (Chef's salad)	1.50

pizza 9''

Fromage (Cheese)	3.25
Pepperoni	3.75
Garnie (All dressed)	4.25

sandwichs
(servis avec frites et salade de choux)
(served with French fries and cole slaw)

Salade aux oeufs (Egg salad)	2.00
Jambon (Ham)	2.50
Poulet (Chicken)	2.25
Tomates et bacon (Tomato & bacon)	2.50
Croque Monsieur	3.25

desserts

Salade de fruits (Fruit salad)	1.25
Tartes (Pies)	1.00
Gâteau moka (Mocha cake)	1.50
Gâteau Forêt Noire (Black Forest cake)	1.75

URB
p. 161

Nom _____

Classe _____ Date _____

Discovering
FRENCH
Nouveau!

BLEU

Unité 2
Resources

Workbook TE
Reading and Culture Activities

B. Agenda

Look at the following page from Stéphanie's pocket calendar.

- What does Stéphanie have scheduled for Saturday morning at 10 A.M.?
  a piano lesson

- When is Stéphanie going to meet Jean-Paul?
  at 4:00 p.m.

- What is Stéphanie planning to do at 7:30?
  She's going to telephone Christine.

Nom _____

Classe _____ Date _____

Discovering
FRENCH *Nouveau!*

BLEU

Unité 2
Resources

Workbook TE
Reading and Culture Activities

C. Les boutiques du Palais des Congrès

In this ad, the shops at the Paris Convention Center (**le Palais des Congrès**) are announcing a large sale. Look at the ad carefully.

- What is the French word for *sale*?

  soldes

- On what day does the sale begin?

  June 19

- On what day does the sale end?

  July 5

- Is there parking available? *yes*

- For how many cars? *1500*

D. « Un bon patriote »

Look at this Paris ticket for "Un bon patriote."

- Where is the performance being held?

  Théâtre National de l'Odéon

- How much does the ticket cost?

  13 euros

- What is the date on the ticket?

  February 22, 2004

- What day of the week is the performance?

  Tuesday

- What time does the performance begin?

  8:00 P.M.

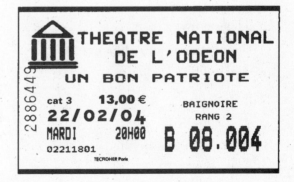

Discovering
FRENCH *Nouveau!*

BLEU

E. La météo

La météo en bref:
23 avril

En Bretagne et en
Normandie, il pleut.

Dans la région parisienne,
il fait beau.

Dans les Alpes, il fait frais.

Cependant sur la Côte d'Azur,
à Nice et à Cannes, il fait
du vent.

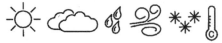

1. What is the weather like in Brittany and Normandy?
   - ❑ It's sunny.
   - ❑ It's windy.
   - ☑ It's rainy.
   - ❑ It's snowing.

2. What is the weather like in Paris?
   - ☑ It's sunny.
   - ❑ It's windy.
   - ❑ It's rainy.
   - ❑ It's snowing.

3. What is the weather like in Nice?
   - ❑ It's sunny.
   - ☑ It's windy.
   - ❑ It's rainy.
   - ❑ It's snowing.

Nom _____

Classe _____ Date _____

Discovering
FRENCH
Nouveau!

BLEU

FORM A

Unité 2 Resources
Unit Test Form A

UNIT TEST 2 (Lessons 3, 4)

Part I. Listening Comprehension

1. The Logical Answer (20 points)

You will hear a series of ten questions. Listen carefully to each question and select the most logical answer on your test sheet. Circle the corresponding letter: a, b, or c. You will hear each question twice.

Modèle: [Tu es française, Christine?]
       a. Oui, ça va.
       b. Oui, j'ai faim.
       c. Oui, je suis de Paris.

1. a. Oui, s'il vous plaît.
  b. Ça fait 30 euros.
  c. Je voudrais un sandwich au fromage.

2. a. Non, merci.
  b. Un soda, s'il te plaît.
  c. Voici une crêpe.

3. a. Oui, j'ai faim.
  b. Oui, donne-moi une limonade.
  c. Oui, il fait beau aujourd'hui.

4. a. Il fait frais.
  b. Oui, je voudrais un croissant.
  c. Ça fait quinze euros.

5. a. Oui, ça va.
  b. Vingt euros, monsieur.
  c. Prête-moi trente euros.

6. a. Il coûte huit euros.
  b. Elle coûte deux euros.
  c. Voici la glace.

7. a. Il fait froid.
  b. Ça fait trente euros.
  c. C'est le 21 décembre.

8. a. Non, il pleut.
  b. Oui, il fait mauvais.
  c. Oui, j'ai faim.

9. a. Merci.
  b. Mercredi.
  c. Juillet.

10. a. Oui, c'est mon anniversaire.
  b. J'ai treize ans.
  c. Le quinze septembre.

2. The Right Time (12 points)

You will hear a French speaker giving the time. Listen carefully and draw in the hands of the clock on your answer sheet. You will hear each time spoken twice.

Modèle:

A.

B.

C.

D.

E.

F.

Nom _____

Classe _____ Date _____ _____

3. The Right Weather (12 points)

You will hear a French speaker describing the weather. Listen carefully and write the corresponding number under the appropriate drawing on your answer sheet. You will hear each weather expression spoken twice.

Modèle:

 _____

Il fait frais.

1.   **2.**   **3.**   **4.**   **5.**   **6.**

_____   _____   _____   _____   _____   _____

Part II. Language and Communication

4. The Right Choice (20 points)

Choose the word or expression that best completes each of the following sentences and circle the corresponding letter: a, b, or c.

1. J'ai faim. Je voudrais _____.
   a. un sandwich
   b. une limonade
   c. un jus d'orange

2. S'il te plaît, prête-moi _____.
   a. vingt euros
   b. un hamburger
   c. un chocolat

3. J'ai soif. Donnez-moi _____, s'il vous plaît.
   a. un croissant
   b. un jus de pomme
   c. un steak-frites

4. Catherine, donne-moi un soda, _____
   a. merci
   b. s'il te plaît
   c. s'il vous plaît

5. _____ combien, s'il vous plaît?
   a. C'est
   b. Il est
   c. Ça va

6. Le sandwich _____ 3 euros.
   a. est
   b. a
   c. coûte

7. Il pleut. _____ mauvais.
   a. Il est
   b. Il fait
   c. Il a

8. _____ été, il fait beau.
   a. Au
   b. En
   c. Il

9. _____ est une saison.
   a. L'hiver
   b. Le mercredi
   c. Septembre

10. _____ fait-il aujourd'hui?
    a. Quel temps
    b. Quelle heure
    c. Quel âge

Nom _____

Classe _____ Date _____

Discovering FRENCH *Nouveau!*

B L E U

Unité 2 Resources

Unit Test Form A

5. The French Calendar (16 points)

Complete the following lists by writing in the missing days and months.

les jours

lundi
mardi
_____
_____
vendredi
_____
dimanche

les mois

_____
_____
mars
_____
mai
juin
_____
août
septembre
_____
novembre
décembre

Part III. Cultural Awareness

6. Culture (20 points)

Choose the completion that reflects the cultural information you have read about in this unit. Circle the corresponding letter: a, b, or c.

1. A French **café** is a place . . .
    a. that serves only coffee.
    b. where you can only order beverages.
    c. where French young people like to get together.

2. In a French **café**, the tip is . . .
    a. never more than 5%.
    b. included in the check.
    c. paid directly to the server.

3. A **croissant** is . . .
    a. a soft drink.
    b. a candy bar.
    c. a type of pastry.

4. In a **café**, a French teenager who is a vegetarian would order . . .
    a. **une crêpe**.
    b. **un sandwich au jambon**.
    c. **un steak-frites**.

5. The **euro** is divided into . . .
    a. 10 **cents** (or **centimes**).
    b. 50 **cents** (or **centimes**).
    c. 100 **cents** (or **centimes**).

6. Euro bank notes have pictures of . . .
    a. windows and bridges.
    b. famous writers and artists.
    c. famous kings and queens.

7. If you order a **steak-frites** in France, you will get . . .
    a. steak and French fries.
    b. steak and baked potato.
    c. steak and fried onion rings.

8. You would go to an **auberge de campagne** (*country inn*) to sample . . .
    a. hearty regional food.
    b. exquisite and expensive cuisine.
    c. a vegetarian menu.

9. *Jacques a dit* is a French version of . . .
    a. "Cops and Robbers."
    b. "Simon Says."
    c. "Jack and Jill."

10. The French-Canadian folk song *Alouette* is about . . .
    a. an eagle.
    b. an owl.
    c. a lark.

Nom _____

Classe _____ Date _____

UNIT TEST 2 (Lessons 3, 4)   **FORM B**

Part I. Listening Comprehension

1. The Logical Answer (20 points)

You will hear a series of ten questions. Listen carefully to each question and select the most logical answer on your test sheet. Circle the corresponding letter: a, b, or c. You will hear each question twice.

Modèle: [Tu es française, Christine?]
      a. Oui, ça va.
      b. Oui, j'ai faim.
      c. Oui, je suis de Paris.

1. a. Oui, s'il te plaît.
   b. Oui, il fait beau.
   c. Oui, donne-moi un sandwich.

2. a. Non, il fait mauvais.
   b. Non, merci.
   c. Oui, donne-moi un soda, s'il te plaît.

3. a. Une glace, s'il te plaît.
   b. Oui, j'ai soif.
   c. Oui, à demain.

4. a. C'est trente euros.
   b. Donnez-moi une limonade.
   c. Non, j'ai faim.

5. a. Il coûte trois euros.
   b. Elle coûte quatre euros.
   c. Oui, j'ai soif.

6. a. Oui, ça va bien.
   b. Comme ci, comme ça.
   c. Vingt-cinq euros, mademoiselle.

7. a. Oui, ça va.
   b. Non, il fait mauvais.
   c. Oui, je suis canadien.

8. a. Très bien, merci.
   b. Il fait chaud.
   c. C'est mercredi.

9. a. Merci.
   b. Demain.
   c. Samedi.

10. a. C'est le premier avril.
    b. Il est dix heures et demie.
    c. Oui, j'ai un rendez-vous.

2. The Right Time (12 points)

You will hear a French speaker giving the time. Listen carefully and draw in the hands of the clock on your answer sheet. You will hear each time spoken twice.

Modèle:

A.

B.

C.

D.

E.

F.

Nom _____

Classe _____ Date _____

3. The Right Weather (12 points)

You will hear a French speaker describing the weather. Listen carefully and write the corresponding number under the appropriate drawing on your answer sheet. You will hear each weather expression spoken twice.

Modèle:

Il fait frais. _____

1.   **2.**   **3.**   **4.**   **5.**   **6.**

Part II. Language and Communication

4. The Right Choice (20 points)

Choose the word or expression that best completes each of the following sentences and circle the corresponding letter: a, b, or c.

1. S'il te plaît, prête-moi _____.
   a. une glace
   b. deux sandwichs
   c. dix euros

2. J'ai soif. Je voudrais _____.
   a. un jus de pomme
   b. un sandwich au jambon
   c. un steak-frites

3. J'ai faim. S'il te plaît, donne-moi _____.
   a. une limonade
   b. un croissant
   c. un jus de raisin

4. Monsieur, donnez-moi un café, _____.
   a. merci
   b. s'il te plaît
   c. s'il vous plaît

5. Ça _____ combien?
   a. fait
   b. va
   c. va bien

6. Voici une glace. _____ coûte deux euros.
   a. Il
   b. Elle
   c. C'est

7. En hiver, il _____ froid.
   a. a
   b. est
   c. fait

8. _____ printemps, il fait frais.
   a. Le
   b. Au
   c. En

9. _____ est une saison.
   a. L'été
   b. Samedi
   c. Juillet

10. _____ fait-il en octobre?
    a. Quel âge
    b. Quel temps
    c. Quelle heure

Nom _____

Classe _____ Date _____

5. The French Calendar (16 points)

Complete the following lists by writing in the missing days and months.

les jours
lundi
_____
mercredi
_____
vendredi
samedi
_____

les mois
janvier
février
_____
avril
_____
_____
juillet
août
_____
octobre
novembre
_____

Part III. Cultural Awareness

6. Culture (20 points)

Choose the completion that reflects the cultural information you have read about in this unit. Circle the corresponding letter: a, b, or c.

1. The **euro** is worth . . .
   a. 10 **cents**.
   b. 50 **cents**.
   c. 100 **cents**.

2. Euro paper money has pictures of . . .
   a. great military leaders.
   b. bridges and doorways.
   c. European animals.

3. In France a **café** is a place . . .
   a. reserved for clients over 21 years old.
   b. where one can buy coffee beans.
   c. where French teenagers get together with their friends.

4. In a French **café**, you can usually order . . .
   a. fish and chips.
   b. different types of sandwiches.
   c. fresh fruits and vegetables.

5. As a beverage, French teenagers often order . . .
   a. milk.
   b. root beer.
   c. fruit juice.

6. You would go to a **boulangerie** or **pâtisserie** in France to buy . . .
   a. pizza.
   b. croissants.
   c. sandwiches.

7. if you order a **steak-frites** in France, you will get . . .
   a. steak and French fries.
   b. steak and fried onion rings.
   c. a steak sandwich.

8. You would go to a **restaurant trois-étoiles** (*three-star restaurant*) to sample . . .
   a. hearty regional food.
   b. exquisite and expensive cuisine.
   c. Vietnamese food.

9. The French game ***Jacques a dit*** is similar to the American game . . .
   a. "Cops and Robbers."
   b. "Simon Says."
   c. "Mother May I."

10. The subject of the French-Canadian folk song ***Alouette*** is a small . . .
    a. seagull.
    b. sparrow.
    c. lark.

Nom _____

Classe _____ Date _____

Discovering
FRENCH
Nouveau!

BLEU

Unité 2
Resources

Unité 2
Listening Comprehension
Performance Test

UNITÉ 2 Listening Comprehension Performance Test

Partie A. Conversations

This part of the Listening Comprehension Test will let you see how well you understand spoken French. You will hear four short conversations. Look at your Listening Comprehension Test Sheet and read the corresponding questions. After you have heard each conversation the second time, select the correct answer and mark the corresponding letter (a, b, c, or d) on your answer sheet.

1. Listen to the following conversation.
   Where did this conversation most likely take place?
   a. at home
   b. in a restaurant
   c. at the school cafeteria
   d. at a hot dog stand

2. Listen to the following conversation between a woman and a man.
   What does the woman want to do?
   a. go to a café
   b. order a sandwich
   c. pay the bill
   d. complain about the food

3. Thomas is phoning Sophie to find out when the movie is. Listen to the conversation.
   What time is the movie?
   a. at 2
   b. at 2:10
   c. at 2:15
   d. at 2:40

4. Listen to the following conversation between Isabelle and Jérôme.
   What are they talking about?
   a. exams
   b. birthdays
   c. weekend plans
   d. summer vacation

5. Listen to the following conversation between Marc and Sophie.
   What are Sophie and Marc talking about?
   a. spring vacation
   b. summer vacation
   c. the weather forecast for this weekend
   d. the weather in general

Nom _____

Classe _____ Date _____

Discovering
FRENCH
Nouveau!

B L E U

Partie B. Questions et réponses

This part of the Listening Comprehension Test will let you see how well you can handle French questions. You will hear Valérie ask several people questions. Listen carefully. Then look at your Listening Comprehension Test Sheet and select the MOST LOGICAL answer to the question you heard. Mark the corresponding letter (a, b, c, or d) on your answer sheet. You will hear each question twice.

6. Valérie is phoning her Uncle Robert in Paris.
   He replies:
   a. Oui, il pleut.
   b. Oui, ça va.
   c. Non, ça va mal.
   d. Oui, il fait bon.

7. This morning Valérie is phoning Julien.
   He replies:
   a. Il est deux heures.
   b. Il fait beau.
   c. Ça fait trente euros.
   d. C'est le 3 mars.

8. Now Valérie and Julien are at an outdoor concert.
   He replies:
   a. Oui, j'ai soif.
   b. Oui, il fait froid.
   c. Ça fait vingt euros.
   d. Oui, donne-moi un sandwich, s'il te plaît.

9. Valérie is at a café.
   The person replies:
   a. Quinze euros, mademoiselle.
   b. Comme ci, comme ça.
   c. Ça va bien. Merci.
   d. S'il vous plaît.

10. Valérie has one last question.
    Her friend replies:
    a. C'est le 3 juillet.
    b. Oui, c'est une copine.
    c. Au revoir! À mardi!
    d. Oui, j'ai un rendez-vous.

Nom _____

Classe _____ Date _____

Discovering
FRENCH
Nouveau!

B L E U

Unité 2
Resources

Speaking Performance Test

UNITÉ 2 Speaking Performance Test

1. Conversations

In this part of the Speaking Performance Test, I will describe a situation and then ask you some related questions. In your answers, use the vocabulary and structures you have learned. Use your imagination.

CONVERSATION A   **UNITÉ 2**

I am your French pen pal, and you are visiting me in Versailles. We have been touring the town, and I am getting hungry. Please answer my questions.

- J'ai faim. Et toi?
- Je veux un steak-frites. Et toi, qu'est-ce que tu veux?
- Je voudrais une salade aussi. Et toi?
- Tu veux une glace ou une crêpe?

CONVERSATION B   **UNITÉ 2**

I am a French friend, and you are visiting me in Nice. We are spending the day at the beach, and it is getting very hot. Please answer my questions.

- J'ai soif. Et toi?
- Je voudrais une limonade. Et toi, qu'est-ce que tu veux?
- Je voudrais une glace aussi. Et toi?
- Tu veux une glace à la vanille ou une glace au chocolat?

CONVERSATION C   **UNITÉ 2**

I am from France and plan to visit the United States. I want to know how much certain things cost in your town. Please answer my questions.

- Combien coûte un hamburger? Un dollar? Deux dollars?
- Combien coûte un soda? Cinquante cents? Un dollar?
- Combien coûte une glace?
- Combien coûte une pizza?

CONVERSATION D   UNITÉ 2

We made several plans for Saturday, but I have forgotten
the times we decided on. Please answer my questions.
(Use your imagination, but be logical.)

- À quelle heure est le match de football?
- À quelle heure est le match de tennis?
- À quelle heure est le dîner?
- À quelle heure est le film?

CONVERSATION E   UNITÉ 2

I have this great calendar watch, but I seem to have
misplaced it. I feel quite lost without knowing the date
and the time. Please help me out.

- Quelle heure est-il?
- Quel jour est-ce aujourd'hui?
- Quelle est la date?
- Et demain, quel jour est-ce?

CONVERSATION F   UNITÉ 2

I am from France and want to know what the weather is
like in the United States. Here are my questions. (Use your
imagination if you are not sure of the answers.)

- Quel temps fait-il à New York en automne?
- Quel temps fait-il à Denver en hiver?
- Quel temps fait-il à San Diego en été?
- Quel temps fait-il à Atlanta au printemps?

Nom _____

Classe _____ Date _____

Discovering FRENCH *Nouveau!*

B L E U

Unité 2 Resources

Speaking Performance Test

2. Tu as la parole

In this part of the Speaking Performance Test, you have the opportunity to make three comments about a familiar topic. Use only the structures and vocabulary you know. Use your imagination.

TU AS LA PAROLE (A)   UNITÉ 2

You are in a restaurant with your friend Hélène. Tell her that . . .

- you are hungry
- you would like a pizza
- you would like a salad too

TU AS LA PAROLE (B)   UNITÉ 2

You are in a French café.

- Call the waitress.
- Tell her that you would like a glass of orange juice.
- Ask her how much it costs.

TU AS LA PAROLE (C)   UNITÉ 2

You are at the home of your French friend Nicolas.

- Tell him that you are thirsty.
- Ask him to please give you a soda.
- Thank him.

Nom _____

Classe _____ Date _____

TU AS LA PAROLE (D)   UNITÉ 2

We had planned to see a tennis match, then meet friends for dinner, and afterwards go to a concert. I have forgotten what times we decided on. Please consult your notebook (below) and let me know at what time each activity is scheduled.

- le match de tennis — 3h15
- le dîner — 5h45
- le concert — 7h30

TU AS LA PAROLE (E)   UNITÉ 2

Name THREE dates that are important to you. You might use the dates listed below or give some other of your own.

- ton anniversaire
- l'anniversaire d'un copain
- l'anniversaire d'une copine

TU AS LA PAROLE (F)   UNITÉ 2

Your French pen pal Sylvie is planning to visit you one day. She wants to know about the weather. Tell her . . .

- how the weather is in winter
- how the weather is in summer
- how the weather is today

Nom _____

Classe _____ Date _____ _____

Discovering FRENCH *Nouveau!*

BLEU

Unité 2 Resources
Reading Comprehension
Performance Test

UNITÉ 2 Reading Comprehension Performance Test

Look at the following ad from a French newspaper. Then read the question. On your Answer Sheet, mark the correct answer by placing a check next to the corresponding letter.

spécialités italiennes
au 1ᵉʳ étage SALONS pour GROUPES et SEMINAIRES
salles climatisées
25, rue MARBEUF   92, av. CH.-DE-GAULLE
CH-ELYSEES (Park. r. François-Iᵉʳ)   NEUILLY
OUVERT jusqu'à 1 h du MATIN 01.47.23.94.23   01.46.37.55.88

1. What would you expect to find on the menu of this restaurant?
   a. crepes
   b. spaghetti
   c. hamburgers

Look at the following ad from a French newspaper. Then read the question. On your Answer Sheet, mark the correct answer by placing a check next to the corresponding letter.

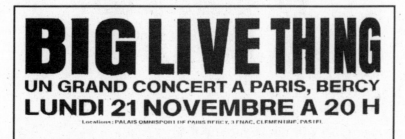

BIG LIVE THING
UN GRAND CONCERT A PARIS, BERCY
LUNDI 21 NOVEMBRE A 20 H
Locations: PALAIS OMNISPORT DE PARIS BERCY, 3 FNAC, CLEMENTINE, PASTEL

2. On what day of the week is this concert going to take place?
   a. Monday
   b. Friday
   c. Saturday

Nom _____

Classe _____ Date _____

Discovering
FRENCH
Nouveau

BLEU

Look at the following ad, which appeared in a Paris weekly. Then read the questions. On your Answer Sheet, mark the correct answers by placing a check next to the corresponding letter.

3. This ad is of interest to people who like . . .
   a. Vietnamese food.
   b. South American costumes.
   c. African music and dance.

4. This event takes place during the month of . . .
   a. January.
   b. June.
   c. July.

Look at the following invitation. Then read the questions. On your Answer Sheet, mark the correct answers by placing a check next to the corresponding letter.

5. For what day of the week is the invitation?
   a. Tuesday
   b. Thursday
   c. Saturday

6. When are the guests expected to arrive?
   a. for lunch
   b. before dinner
   c. after dinner

7. Why is Béatrice inviting people?
   a. to listen to Jean-Claude's rock band
   b. to celebrate her parents' anniversary
   c. to celebrate her brother's birthday

Nom _____

Classe _____ Date _____

Look at the following weather forecast from a French newspaper. Then read the questions. On your Answer Sheet, mark the correct answers by placing a check next to the corresponding letter.

LA MÉTÉO
Samedi 28 mars

- froid dans le Nord de la France
- beau temps dans l'Ouest et le Centre
- chaud en Provence
- importantes chutes de neige dans les Alpes

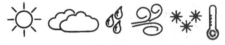

8. This is the weather forecast for . . .
   a. a spring day
   b. a winter weekend
   c. a week in summer

9. In which area of France will the weather be the warmest?
   a. in the North
   b. in the West
   c. in Provence

10. Where would you go if you wanted to ski on fresh snow?
   a. to Provence
   b. to the Alps
   c. to Central France

Nom _____

Classe _____ Date _____

Discovering
FRENCH
Nouveau!

B L E U

Unité 2
Resources

Writing Performance Test

UNITÉ 2 Writing Performance Test

A. Au café (15 points)

Write the names of three foods and two beverages that you could order in a French café.
Use **un** or **une** as appropriate. Use the pictures below as a guide or choose other items.

NOURRITURES

- _____

- _____

- _____

BOISSONS

- _____

- _____

B. Le pique-nique (20 points)

Jean-Pierre has invited you to a picnic.

- Tell him that you are thirsty.   «_____»

- Ask him to please give you a soda.   «_____»

- Tell him that you are hungry.   «_____»

- Ask him to give you a hamburger.   «_____»

Nom _____

Classe _____ Date _____

C. Quelle heure est-il? (50 points)

Write out the times in French.

_____

_____

_____

_____

Nom _____

Classe _____ Date _____

Discovering
FRENCH *Nouveau!*

B L E U

Unité 2
Resources

Writing Performance Test

D. Questions (30 points)

Answer the following questions in full sentences.

1. Quel jour est-ce aujourd'hui?

_____

2. Quel jour est-ce demain?

_____

3. Quelle est la date?

_____

4. Quel âge as-tu?

_____

5. C'est quand, ton anniversaire?

_____

6. C'est quand, l'anniversaire de ton copain?

_____

Discovering
FRENCH
Nouveau!

B L E U

Nom _____

Classe _____ Date _____

E. Le temps (15 points)

Your French pen pal André wants to know what the weather is like in your region. Describe your typical weather by completing the following note. Use at least five different weather expressions.

Cher André,

En hiver, _____.

Au printemps, _____.

En été, _____.

En automne, _____.

Aujourd'hui, _____.

Nom _____

Classe _____ Date _____

Discovering
FRENCH
Nouveau!

BLEU

Unité 2
Resources

Multiple Choice Test Items

UNITÉ 2 Multiple Choice Test Items

Leçon 3

1. —Tu as faim?
   —Oui, _____
   a. qu'est-ce que tu veux?
   b. j'ai seize ans.
   c. je voudrais un sandwich.

2. Qu'est-ce que tu veux?
   Un _____, s'il te plaît.
   a. croissant
   b. pizza
   c. omelette

3. _____ une glace.
   a. J'ai faim
   b. S'il te plaît
   c. Je voudrais

4. Tu veux une _____?
   a. steak
   b. salade
   c. hot dog

5. Qu'est-ce que tu veux? Une crêpe ou une _____?
   a. glace
   b. sandwich
   c. croissant

6. S'il te plaît, donne-moi _____ pizza.
   a. un
   b. une
   c. l'

7. Mademoiselle, vous désirez?
   _____ une limonade, s'il vous plaît.
   a. Donne-moi
   b. J'ai soif
   c. Donnez-moi

8. Tu veux un thé?
   Non, merci, donne-moi un soda, _____.
   a. s'il vous plaît
   b. s'il te plaît
   c. je voudrais

9. Tu as soif?
   Oui, je voudrais une _____.
   a. limonade
   b. jus de pomme
   c. crêpe

10. Monsieur, s'il vous plaît!
    _____?
    Donnez-moi un sandwich, s'il vous plaît.
    a. Tu as faim
    b. Tu as soif
    c. Vous désirez

11. Vous désirez?
    Je voudrais un hamburger et un _____.
    a. soda
    b. limonade
    c. glace

12. —Tu as faim?
    —Non, _____.
    a. j'ai soif. Je voudrais un jus de tomate
    b. je voudrais un steak-frites, s'il te plaît
    c. donnez-moi un sandwich, s'il vous plaît

13. Un sandwich et un café, _____?
    a. ça fait combien
    b. combien coûte
    c. vous désirez

14. Combien coûte le chocolat?
    _____ deux euros cinquante.
    a. Voici
    b. Il coûte
    c. Tu veux

15. Le sandwich coûte quatre euros et le café coûte deux euros. _____ six euros.
    a. Ça fait
    b. Il coûte
    c. Elle coûte

16. Voici un jus de raisin. _____ coûte combien?
    a. Il
    b. Elle
    c. Le

17. Voilà _____. Il coûte huit euros.
    a. une pizza
    b. un steak-frites
    c. une salade

18. You are in a pastry shop with a friend. You would like to order ice cream. It costs three euros. You have two euros in your pocket. What do you say to your friend?
    a. Donnez-moi deux euros, s'il vous plaît.
    b. Il coûte deux euros.
    c. Prête-moi un euro, s'il te plaît.

Nom _____

Classe _____ Date _____

Discovering
FRENCH
Nouveau!

BLEU

Unité 2
Resources

Multiple Choice Test Items

Read the following menu and the statements that follow. Choose the answers that best complete these statements.

BOISSONS CHAUDES

Café . . . . .1 euro

Chocolat . . . . .2 euros

Thé . . . . .1, 5 euros

Soda . . . . .1, 5 euros

BOISSONS FRAÎCHES

Limonade . . . . .1,5 euros

Jus d'orange . . . . .2 euros

Jus de tomate . . . . .2 euros

SANDWICHS

Hot dog . . . . .2 euros

Hamburger . . . . .3 euros

Autres sandwichs . . . . .2, 5 euros

Salade verte . . . . .5 euros

Glace . . . . .3 euros

PLATS DIVERS

Steak-frites . . . . .8 euros

Crêpe . . . . .4 euros

Omelette . . . . .4 euros

---

19. At this café, there are _____ different things to drink.
    a. 7
    b. 3
    c. 8

20. You are ordering eggs and a cup of coffee. When the waiter comes, you ask him: "*Ça fait combien?*" What does he answer?
    a. Il coûte cinq euros.
    b. Ça fait cinq euros.
    c. Voilà cinq euros.

Nom _____

Classe _____ Date _____

Discovering
FRENCH
Nouveau!

BLEU

Leçon 4

Look at the page in Noëlle's agenda. Choose the best answer for the three questions that follow.

Samedi, 12 novembre

8 h 30: Yoga

12 h: Rendez-vous avec David – Restaurant "Le steak-frites"

5 h: Thé avec Mme Dufour

8 h: Cinéma avec Patricia

1. At what time is Noëlle's yoga class?
   a. à neuf heures trente
   b. à huit heures et quart
   c. à huit heures et demie

2. What time is it when Noëlle meets Patricia?
   a. Il est huit heures du matin.
   b. Il est huit heures de l'après-midi.
   c. Il est huit heures du soir.

3. What time is it when Noëlle meets David for lunch?
   a. Il est onze heures.
   b. Il est midi.
   c. Il est minuit.

4. Noëlle meets Madame Dufour for a cup of tea and answers "Il est cinq heures." What was Madame Dufour's question?
   a. Quelle heure est-il?
   b. À quelle heure est le thé?
   c. Quel jour est-ce?

5. Today's date is Saturday, November 12. On what day of the week does November 13 fall?
   a. mercredi
   b. vendredi
   c. dimanche

6. Today's date is Saturday, November 12. Noëlle's birthday is in exactly two months. When is her birthday?
   a. le 12 juin
   b. le 12 janvier
   c. le 12 juillet

7. Noëlle's birthday is on January 12. She lives in the northern part of France. Most likely, what is the weather like on her birthday?
   a. Il fait bon.
   b. Il fait chaud.
   c. Il fait froid.

Nom _____

Classe _____ Date _____ _____

Discovering FRENCH Nouveau!

BLEU

Unité 2 Resources

Multiple Choice Test Items

8. Noëlle's birthday is on January 12. In what season is Noëlle's birthday?
   a. en automne
   b. au printemps
   c. en hiver

9. Quelle heure est-il?
   a. trois euros
   b. C'est le deux mars.
   c. Il est dix heures.

10. Continue the series: huit heures, huit heures et quart, _____
   a. huit heures moins le quart
   b. neuf heures moins le quart
   c. huit heures et demie

11. Continue the series: deux heures de l'après-midi, une heure de l'après-midi, _____
   a. douze heures de l'après-midi
   b. minuit
   c. midi

12. À quelle heure est le film?
   Le film est _____.
   a. huit heures
   b. huit jours
   c. à huit heures

13. mardi, mercredi, _____
   a. lundi
   b. jeudi
   c. vendredi

14. Aujourd'hui, c'est jeudi. À demain!
   Oui, _____!
   a. à vendredi
   b. à mercredi
   c. dimanche

15. _____?
   C'est lundi.
   a. Quelle heure est-il?
   b. Quel jour est-il?
   c. Quel jour est-ce?

16. dimanche le trois février, samedi le deux février, vendredi le _____ février
   a. un
   b. vingt-huit
   c. premier

17. C'est quand, ton anniversaire?
   a. Il est le premier avril.
   b. C'est le deux septembre.
   c. Il est trois heures.

18. Which comes first?
    a. le 5 juin
    b. le 13 mars
    c. le premier mai

19. Il neige _____.
    a. au printemps
    b. en été
    c. en hiver

20. En été, _____.
    a. il fait chaud
    b. il fait mauvais
    c. il fait froid

Nom _____

Classe _____ Date _____ _____

Discovering
FRENCH
Nouveau!

B L E U

Unité 2
Resources

Test Scoring Tools

UNITÉ 2 Listening Comprehension Performance Test Answer Sheet

A. Conversations

1. a. ___   2. a. ___   3. a. ___   4. a. ___
   b. ___   b. ___   b. ___   b. ___
   c. ___   c. ___   c. ___   c. ___
   d. ___   d. ___   d. ___   d. ___

B. Questions et réponses

5. a. ___   6. a. ___   7. a. ___   8. a. ___   9. a. ___   10. a. ___
   b. ___   b. ___   b. ___   b. ___   b. ___   b. ___
   c. ___   c. ___   c. ___   c. ___   c. ___   c. ___
   d. ___   d. ___   d. ___   d. ___   d. ___   d. ___

UNITÉ 2 Reading Comprehension Performance Test Answer Sheet

1. a. ___   2. a. ___   3. a. ___   4. a. ___   5. a. ___
   b. ___   b. ___   b. ___   b. ___   b. ___
   c. ___   c. ___   c. ___   c. ___   c. ___

6. a. ___   7. a. ___   8. a. ___   9. a. ___   10. a. ___
   b. ___   b. ___   b. ___   b. ___   b. ___
   c. ___   c. ___   c. ___   c. ___   c. ___

UNIT TEST 2 (Lessons 3, 4)

FORM A

Part I. Listening Comprehension

CD 13, Track 15

1. The Logical Answer (20 points)

You will hear a series of ten questions. Listen carefully to each question and select the most logical answer on your test sheet. Circle the corresponding letter: a, b, or c. You will hear each question twice. First listen to the model.

Modèle: Tu es française, Christine?
You should have circled the letter "**c**": **Oui, je suis de Paris.**

Let's begin. Écoutez.

1. Vous désirez?
2. Qu'est-ce que tu veux?
3. Tu as soif?
4. Tu as faim?
5. Ça fait combien?
6. Combien coûte la glace?
7. Quel temps fait-il en hiver?
8. Il fait beau?
9. Quel jour est-ce?
10. C'est quand ton anniversaire?

CD 13, Track 16

2. The Right Time (12 points)

You will hear a French speaker giving the time. Listen carefully and draw in the hands of the clock on your answer sheet. You will hear each time spoken twice. First listen to the model.

Modèle: Il est trois heures.

You should have draw the hands in the position for "three o'clock."

Let's begin. Écoutez.

A. Il est deux heures dix.
B. Il est onze heures.
C. Il est une heure et quart.

D. Il est dix heures moins cinq.
E. Il est neuf heures et demie.
F. Il est minuit.

CD 13, Track 17

3. The Right Weather (12 points)

You will hear a French speaker describing the weather. Listen carefully and write the corresponding letter next to the appropriate drawing on your answer sheet. You will hear each weather expression spoken twice. First listen to the model.

Modèle: A. Il fait frais.

You should have written an "A" next to the picture of cool weather.

Let's begin. Écoutez.

B. Il fait beau.
C. Il neige.
D. Il fait froid.

E. Il fait chaud.
F. Il pleut.
G. Il fait mauvais.

Discovering
FRENCH
Nouveau!

BLEU

Unité 2
Resources

Audioscripts

UNIT TEST 2 (Lessons 3, 4)

FORM B

Part I. Listening Comprehension

CD 13, Track 18

1. The Logical Answer (20 points)

You will hear a series of ten questions. Listen carefully to each question and select the most logical answer on your test sheet. Circle the corresponding letter: a, b, or c. You will hear each question twice. First listen to the model.

Modèle: Tu es française, Christine?
You should have circled the letter **"c": Oui, je suis de Paris.**

Let's begin. Écoutez.

1. Tu as faim?
2. Tu as soif?
3. Qu'est-ce que tu veux?
4. Vous désirez?
5. Combien coûte le jus de pomme?
6. Ça fait combien?
7. Il fait beau à Québec?
8. Quel temps fait-il aujourd'hui?
9. Quel jour est-ce aujourd'hui?
10. Quelle est la date?

CD 13, Track 19

2. The Right Time (12 points)

You will hear a French speaker giving the time. Listen carefully and draw in the hands of the clock on your answer sheet. You will hear each time spoken twice. First listen to the model.

Modèle: Il est trois heures.
You should have drawn the hands in the position for "three o'clock."

Let's begin. Écoutez.

A. Il est cinq heures vingt.
B. Il est deux heures et quart.
C. Il est une heure et demie.
D. Il est midi.
E. Il est sept heures moins le quart.
F. Il est huit heures moins dix.

CD 13, Track 20

3. The Right Weather (12 points)

You will hear a French speaker describing the weather. Listen carefully and write the corresponding letter next to the appropriate drawing on your answer sheet. You will hear each weather expression spoken twice. First listen to the model.

Modèle: A. Il fait frais.

You should have written an "A" next to the picture of cool weather.

Let's begin. Écoutez.

B. Il fait froid.
C. Il pleut.
D. Il fait mauvais.
E. Il fait beau.
F. Il neige.
G. Il fait chaud.

UNITÉ 2   Listening Comprehension Performance Test

Partie A. Conversations

CD 13, Track 21

This part of the Listening Comprehension Test will let you see how well you understand spoken French. You will hear four short conversations. Look at your Listening Comprehension Test Sheet and read the corresponding questions. After you have heard each conversation the second time, select the correct answer and mark the corresponding letter (a, b, c, or d) on your answer sheet.

Let's begin.

1. *Listen to the following conversation.*

   HOMME: Vous désirez, mademoiselle?
   FILLE: Je voudrais un steak-frites.
   HOMME: Et pour vous, monsieur?
   GARÇON: Donnez-moi une omelette et une salade.

2. *Listen to the following conversation between a woman and a man.*

   FEMME: S'il vous plaît, monsieur.
   HOMME: Oui, madame.
   FEMME: Ça fait combien?
   HOMME: Voyons, 5 euros pour le sandwich et 2 euros pour le café . . . Ça fait 7 euros, madame.

3. *Thomas is phoning Sophie to find out when the movie is. Listen to the conversation.*

   THOMAS: Allô, Sophie? Ça va?
   SOPHIE: Oui. Ça va, Thomas.
   THOMAS: Dis, à quelle heure est le film?
   SOPHIE: À deux heures et quart.
   THOMAS: Merci.

4. *Listen to the following conversation between Isabelle and Jérôme.*

   ISABELLE: C'est quand, ton anniversaire?
   JÉRÔME: C'est le 21 octobre. Et toi?
   ISABELLE: Moi, c'est le premier juillet.

5. *Listen to the following conversation between Marc and Sophie.*

   MARC: Quel temps fait-il ici au printemps?
   SOPHIE: Il fait beau.
   MARC: Et en automne?
   SOPHIE: Il pleut et il fait froid.

Partie B. Questions et réponses

CD 13, Track 22

This part of the Listening Comprehension Test will let you see how well you can handle French questions. You will hear Valérie ask several people questions. Listen carefully. Then look at your Listening Comprehension Test Sheet and select the MOST LOGICAL answer to the question you heard. Mark the corresponding letter (a, b, c, or d) on your answer sheet. You will hear each question twice.

Let's begin.

6. *Valérie is phoning her Uncle Robert in Paris. In their conversation, she asks:*
   Il fait mauvais?

7. *This morning Valérie is phoning Julien. She asks:*
   Quel temps fait-il?

8. *Now Valérie and Julien are at an outdoor concert. She asks:*
   Tu as faim?

9. *Valérie is at a café. She asks:*
   Ça fait combien?

10. *Valérie has one last question. She asks:*
    Quelle est la date?

UNITÉ 2 ANSWER KEY

Video Activities

Module 3A Tu as faim? (Pages 38–41)

Activité 1. Dialogue: Tu as faim?
1. une pizza
2. un sandwich
3. une pizza

Activité 2. Tout le monde a faim!
Students should have marked a, c, d, f, g, h, and j.

Activité 3. Je voudrais . . .
1. a
2. a
3. a

Activité 4. Qu'est-ce qu'on mange?
À la boulangerie: bread, croissants, éclair, pain au chocolat, pain aux raisins, une brioche
Dans la rue: pizza, crêpes, hot dog, une saucisse
Au café: un sandwich au jambon, un sandwich au fromage, un sandwich au pâté, un sandwich jambon-gruyère
Question personnelle sample answers:
À la boulangerie: un éclair
Dans la rue: pizza
Au café: un sandwich au jambon

Activité 5. Le goûter
Dialogues will vary.

Module 3B Au café (Pages 42–45)

Activité 1. Dialogue: Au café
1. Trinh
2. Trinh
3. waiter
4. waiter
5. waiter

Activité 2. S'il vous plaît
Students should have marked a, b, d, e, f, g, h, and i once, j twice, and c not at all.

Activité 3. La carte des boissons
 A. *Sample answers:*
un citron pressé: freshly squeezed lemonade (add water)
une orange pressée: freshly squeezed orange juice
une limonade: carbonated drink with lemon flavor
un diabolo-menthe: **limonade** with mint syrup
un diabolo-fraise: **limonade** with strawberry syrup
 B. *Sample answer:* une limonade

Activité 4. Vous désirez?
Scenes will vary.

Module 3C Ça fait combien? (Pages 46–49)

Activité 1. Dialogue: Ça fait combien?
1 jus d'orange: 2 € 50
1 limonade: 1 € 50
total: 4 €

Activité 2. Ça fait combien?
1. b
2. a
3. a
4. b
5. a
6. a
7. b

Activité 3. L'argent français
1. faux
2. vrai
3. faux
4. faux
5. vrai
6. vrai
7. faux

Activité 4. Les billets
1. Il est violet.
2. Il est jaune.
3. Il est vert.
4. Il est orange.
5. Il est bleu.
6. Il est rouge.
7. Il est gris.

Activité 5. Au Restaurant Le Select
Scenes will vary.

Module 4A L'heure (Pages 103–106)

Activité 1. Un rendez-vous
1. — Quelle heure est-il?
2. — Trois heures?
3. — Oh là là! J'ai un rendez-vous avec David dans vingt minutes. Au revoir, Jean-Paul.

Activité 2. L'heure
1. 6:00
2. 8:00
3. 1:00
4. 12:00
5. 11:00
6. 10:00
7. 2:00

Activité 3. L'heure exact
a. (5:30) The minute hand should point to 6.
b. (6:45) The minute hand should point to 9.
c. (4:05) The minute hand should point to 1.
d. (3:50) The minute hand should point to 10.

Activité 4. Dialogue. À quelle heure est le film?
1. et demie
2. et quart

Activité 5. À quelle heure?
1. e
2. c
3. d
4. b
5. f

Activité 6. L'heure officielle
1. 14 h 25
2. 22 h 45
3. 24 h
4. 16 h 15
5. 18 h 30
6. 20 h 10

Question d'opinion
Sample answer: Yes, because there would be no confusion between A.M. and P.M.

Activité 7. Le train
Dialogues:
— À quelle heure est le train d'Orange?
— Le train d'Orange est à dix heures trente.

— À quelle heure est le train d'Avignon?
— Le train d'Avignon est à onze heures cinquante.

— À quelle heure est le train d'Arles?
— Le train d'Arles est à treize heures cinq.

— À quelle heure est le train de Cannes?
— Le train de Cannes est à quinze heures dix.

— À quelle heure est le train d'Antibes?
— Le train d'Antibes est à dix-huit heures quarante-cinq.

— À quelle heure est le train de Nice?
— Le train de Nice est à vingt-deux heures trente.

Module 4B Le jour et la date (Pages 107–110)

Activité 1. A. Dialogues: Quel jour est-ce?
1. vendredi; samedi
2. mercredi; jeudi

Activité 2. B. Deux anniversaires
1. 18
2. 18

Activité 3. Quelle est la date?
1. le trente mars
2. le premier juin
3. le quinze avril
4. le vingt-quatre mai
5. le deux février
6. le vingt-deux mars
7. le trois juin
8. le premier juillet
9. le huit août
10. le trois septembre
11. le quatre novembre

Activité 4. C'est quand, votre anniversaire?
1. juillet
2. décembre
3. mars
4. mai
5. mai
6. novembre
7. janvier

Activité 5. Joyeux anniversaire!
 A. *Sample answer:* I invite a few friends over, we have cake and ice cream, I open my gifts.
 B. 1. birthday cake
 2. happy birthday
 C. *Sample answer:* Philippe didn't have ice cream, and some of the gifts—like an Astérix cartoon book—are different.

Activité 6. C'est quand, ton anniversaire?
Answers will vary.

Module 4C Le temps (Pages 111–114)

Activité 1. Dialogue: Le temps
1. Il fait mauvais!
2. Il pleut.
3. Papa va nous inviter au restaurant.

Activité 2. La date et le temps
1. neige
2. froid
3. frais
4. pleut
5. bon
6. chaud
7. pleut
8. mauvais
9. froid

Activité 3. La géographie de la France
1. vrai
2. faux
3. vrai
4. vrai
5. faux
6. vrai
7. vrai
8. faux
9. faux
10. faux
11. vrai
12. vrai
13. faux

Activité 4. Bonjour, la France!
1. les Vosges
2. l'Alsace
3. la Touraine
4. la Savoie
5. les Alpes
6. le Massif Central
7. la Provence
8. les Pyrénées

Activité 5. Quel temps fait-il?
À Lille . . . il fait frais.
À Strasbourg . . . il pleut (il fait mauvais).
À Paris . . . il pleut (il fait mauvais).
À Nantes . . . il pleut (il fait mauvais).
À Bordeaux . . . il pleut (il fait mauvais).
À Albertville . . . il neige (il fait froid).
À Nice . . . il fait beau (il fait chaud, il fait bon).
À Tours . . . il fait frais.
À Toulouse . . . il fait beau (il fait chaud, il fait bon).
À Marseille . . . il fait beau (il fait chaud, il fait bon).

Lesson Quizzes

Quiz 3

Part I : Listening

A. Conversations (40 points)
1. c
2. a
3. b
4. b
5. c

Part II: Writing

B. En France (30 points)
Answers will vary. Sample answers:
1. une glace
2. une pizza
3. une omelette
4. un hot dog
5. un sandwich
6. un steak

C. Expression personnelle (30 points)
Answers will vary. Sample answers:

- Mademoiselle, j'ai soif.
- S'il vous plaît, donnez-moi un jus de pomme. (Un jus de pomme, s'il vous plaît.)
- C'est combien?
  [Combien coûte le jus de pomme?]

Quiz 4

Part I: Listening

A. Conversations (25 points)

1. 4:00
2. 4:45
3. 12:00
4. 2:30
5. 8:20

B. Conversations (40 points)

1. b
2. c
3. c
4. a
5. c

Part II: Writing

C. Le temps (30 points)

1. Il fait bon. (Il fait beau.)
2. Il fait froid.
3. Il fait mauvais.
4. Il fait frais.
5. Il neige.

D. Expression personnelle (30 points)
Answers will vary. Sample answers:
- Aujourd'hui, c'est mercredi.
- Mon anniversaire est le 21 décembre.

Communipak

Interviews

Interview 1

Je voudrais un sandwich (un hamburger).
Je voudrais une salade (une omelette).
Je voudrais une limonade (un soda).
Je voudrais un jus de pomme (un jus d'orange).

Interview 2

Sample answers:
Oui, ça va bien.
Il est dix heures et demie.
La classe est à dix heures trente-cinq.

Interview 3

Sample answers:
C'est jeudi.
C'est le 10 octobre.
C'est le 15 février.

Interview 4

Sample answers:
C'est mardi.
C'est le 15 novembre.
C'est le premier septembre.

Interview 5

Sample answers:
Il fait mauvais.
Il neige.
Il fait chaud.
Il fait beau.

Tu as la parole

Answers will vary. Sample answers:

Tu as la parole 1

Il fait chaud.
J'ai soif.
Je voudrais un soda.

Tu as la parole 2

Il est midi. J'ai faim.
Je voudrais un hamburger.

Prête-moi 3 euros, s'il te plaît.

Tu as la parole 3

Je voudrais un steak-frites, s'il vous plaît.
Je voudrais un soda, s'il vous plaît.
Ça fait combien?

Tu as la parole 4

un hamburger, un steak
une pizza, une omelette
un café, un limonade

Tu as la parole 5

samedi
mai
printemps

Tu às la parole 6

En hiver, il fait froid à Chicago.
En été, il fait chaud à Miami.
En automne, il fait beau à Boston.

Tu as la parole 7

Aujourd'hui, c'est vendredi.
Il est trois heures et quart.
Il fait beau.

Tu as la parole 8

Mon anniversaire, c'est le 8 septembre.
L'anniversaire de mon copain, c'est le 25 octobre.
L'anniversaire de ma copine, c'est le 23 août.

Conversations Side A

Conversation 1

Tu as soif?
Tu as faim?
Tu veux un sandwich?
Tu veux un soda?

Conversation 2

Sample answers:
Je voudrais un steak (une pizza), s'il te plaît.
Je voudrais une crêpe (une glace), s'il te plaît.
Je voudrais un jus de pomme (un jus d'orange), s'il te plaît.

Conversation 3

Sample answers:
Combien coûte le steak-frites?
Combien coûte la salade?
Prête-moi 10 euros, s'il te plaît.

Conversation 4

Sample answers:
Il fait très froid en hiver.
Il fait beau en automne.
Il fait chaud en été.

Conversation 5

Sample answers:
Quelle heure est-il?
À quelle heure est le dîner?
À quelle heure est le concert?

Conversation 6

Sample answers:
Il est midi.
Le film est à 4h.
Le billet coûte 7€.

Conversation 7

Sample answers:
Quelle heure est-il?
Quel jour est-ce?
Quel temps fait-il?

Conversation 8

Sample answers:
Mon anniversaire, c'est le 8 septembre.

Le dîner est lundi.
Le dîner est à 8h.

Conversations Side B

Conversation 1

Sample answers:
Oui, j'ai soif.
Oui, j'ai faim.
Oui, je voudrais un soda.

Conversation 2

Sample answers:
Tu veux un steak ou une pizza?
Tu veux une crêpe ou une glace?
Tu veux un jus d'orange ou un jus de pomme?

Conversation 3

Sample answers:
Le steak-frites coûte 7 euros.
La salade coûte 3 euros.
Voici 10 euros.

Conversation 4

Sample answers:
Quel temps fait-il en hiver?
Quel temps fait-il en automne?
Quel temps fait-il en été?

Conversation 5

Sample answers:
Il est midi.
Le dîner est à 6h.
Le concert est à 8h.

Conversation 6

Sample answers:
Quelle heure est-il?
À quelle heure est le film?
Combien coûte le billet?

Conversation 7

Sample answers:
Il est 3h.
Aujourd'hui, c'est jeudi.
Il pleut.

Conversation 8

Sample answers:
C'est quand, ton anniversaire?
Quel jour est le dîner?
À quelle heure est le dîner?

Échanges

Échange 1

Answers will vary.

Échange 2

Answers will vary.

Échange 3

Answers will vary.

Échange 4

Sample answers:
Il pleut. Je voudrais un thé.
Il neige. Je voudrais un chocolat.
Il fait froid. Je voudrais un thé.

Tête à tête

Activité 1 Combien coûte . . . ?

Élève A

a.
Combien coûte le café?
Combien coûte la limonade?
Combien coûte le chocolat?
Combien coûte le jus de pomme?

b.

Le hamburger coûte trois euros.
La pizza coûte quatre euros cinquante.
Le steak-frites coûte cinq euros vingt.
La salade coûte deux euros soixante.
La glace coûte deux euros soixante-quinze.

Élève B

a.

Le jus d'orange coûte deux euros.
Le café coûte un euro dix.
La limonade coûte un euro vingt-cinq.
Le chocolat coûte un euro dix.
Le jus de pomme coûte un euro
    soixante-quinze.

b.

Combien coûte une pizza?
Combien coûte un steak-frites?
Combien coûte une salade?
Combien coûte une glace?

Activité 2 À quelle heure?

Élève A

a.

À quelle heure est le match de volley?
À quelle heure est la classe de maths?
À quelle heure est le concert de rock?
À quelle heure est le récital?

b.

Le film est à huit heures.
Le concert de jazz est à quatre heures et demie.
Le dîner est à sept heures et quart.
Le match de tennis est à deux heures quarante-
    cinq (trois heures moins le quart).
La classe de français est à neuf heures
    cinquante-cinq.

Élève B

a.

Le pique-nique est à deux heures.
Le match de volley est à une heure et quart
    (une heure quinze).
La classe de maths est à onze heures vingt.
Le concert de rock est à sept heures
    quarante-cinq (huit heures moins le quart).
Le récital est à quatre heures et demie.

b.

À quelle heure est le concert de jazz?
À quelle heure est le dîner?
À quelle heure est le match de tennis?
À quelle heure est la classe de français?

Activité 3 Joyeux anniversaire!

Élève A

a. *Sample answers:*
le 12 mai
le 2 décembre
le 15 juillet

b.

C'est quand, l'anniversaire de ton cousin?
C'est quand, l'anniversaire de ta copine?

Élève B

a.

C'est quand, l'anniversaire de ton copain?
C'est quand, l'anniversaire de ta mère?

b. *Sample answers:*
le 4 mars
le 18 août
le premier avril

Activité 4 Quel temps fait-il?

Élève A

a.

Quel temps fait-il à Lille?
Quel temps fait-il à Deauville?
Quel temps fait-il à Albertville?
Quel temps fait-il à Bordeaux?

b.

Le hamburger coûte trois euros.

b.

À Québec il fait froid.
À Vancouver il fait beau.
À Toronto il fait mauvais.
À Calgary il neige.
À Montréal il pleut.

Élève B

a.

À Nice il fait chaud.
À Lille il pleut.
À Deauville il fait beau.
À Albertville il neige.
À Bordeaux il fait mauvais.

b.

Quel temps fait-il à Vancouver?
Quel temps fait-il à Toronto?
Quel temps fait-il à Calgary?
Quel temps fait-il à Montréal?

Unit Test Lessons 3, 4

Form A

Part I. Listening Comprehension

1. The Logical Answer (20 points)

1. c	6. b
2. b	7. a
3. b	8. a
4. b	9. b
5. b	10. c

2. The Right Time (12 points)

A. 2:10	D. 9:55
B. 11:00	E. 9:30
C. 1:15	F. 12:00

3. The Right Weather (12 points)

1. b	4. d
2. g	5. f
3. e	6. c

Part II. Language and Communication

4. The Right Choice (20 points)

1. a	6. c
2. a	7. b
3. b	8. b
4. b	9. a
5. a	10. a

5. The French Calendar (16 points)
Les jours: mercredi, jeudi, samedi
Les mois: janvier, février, avril, juillet, octobre

Part III. Cultural Awareness

6. Culture (20 points)

1. c	6. a
2. b	7. a
3. c	8. a
4. a	9. b
5. c	10. c

Form B

Part I. Listening Comprehension

1. The Logical Answer (20 points)

1. c	6. c
2. c	7. b
3. a	8. b
4. b	9. c
5. a	10. a

2. The Right Time (12 points)

A. 5:20	D. 12:00
B. 2:15	E. 6:45
C. 1:30	F. 7:50

3. The Right Weather (12 points)

1. e	4. b
2. d	5. c
3. g	6. f

Part II. Language and Communication

4. The Right Choice (20 points)

1. c	6. b
2. a	7. c
3. b	8. b
4. c	9. a
5. a	10. b

5. The French Calendar (16 points)
Les jours: mardi, jeudi, dimanche
Les mois: mars, mai, juin, septembre,
    décembre

Part III. Cultural Awareness

6. Culture (20 points)

1. c	6. b
2. b	7. a
3. c	8. b
4. b	9. b
5. c	10. c

Listening Comprehension Performance Test

A. Conversations

1. b	4. b
2. c	5. d
3. c	

B. Questions et réponses

6. a	9. a
7. b	10. a
8. d	

Reading Comprehension Performance Test

1. b	6. b
2. a	7. c
3. c	8. a
4. b	9. c
5. b	10. b

Writing Performance Test

Answers will vary. Sample answers:

A. Au café (15 points)
Nourritures
• une salade
• un sandwich
• un steak-frites
Boissons
• un chocolat
• un jus d'orange

B. Le pique-nique (20 points)
• J'ai soif.
• Donne-moi un soda, s'il te plaît.
• J'ai faim.
• Donne-moi un hamburger.

C. Quelle heure est-il? (20 points)
Il est cinq heures dix.
Il est une heure et quart.
Il est huit heures et demie.
Il est neuf heures cinquante-cinq.

D. Questions (30 points)
1. C'est lundi.
2. C'est mardi.
3. C'est le 3 octobre.
4. J'ai treize ans.
5. C'est le premier novembre.
6. C'est le 21 avril.

E. Le temps (15 points)
il fait froid et il neige
il pleut et il fait frais
il fait chaud
il fait bon
il fait mauvais

Multiple Choice Test Items

Leçon 3

1. c. je voudrais un sandwich
2. a. croissant
3. c. Je voudrais
4. b. salade
5. a. glace
6. b. une
7. c. Donnez-moi
8. b. s'il te plaît
9. a. limonade
10. c. Vous désirez
11. a. soda
12. a. j'ai soif. Je voudrais un jus de tomate
13. a. ça fait combien
14. b. Il coûte
15. a. Ça fait
16. a. Il
17. b. un steak-frites
18. c. Prête-moi un euro, s'il te plaît.
19. a. 7
20. b. Ça fait cinq euros.

Leçon 4

1. c. à huit heures et demie
2. c. Il est huit heures du soir.
3. b. Il est midi.
4. a. Quelle heure est-il?
5. c. dimanche
6. b. le 12 janvier
7. c. Il fait froid.
8. c. en hiver
9. c. Il est dix heures.
10. c. huit heures et demie
11. c. midi
12. c. à huit heures
13. b. jeudi
14. a. à vendredi
15. c. Quel jour est-ce?
16. c. premier
17. b. C'est le deux septembre
18. b. le 13 mars
19. c. en hiver
20. a. il fait chaud